Turkish A
The Istanbul Super Connector

JOZEF MOLS

Key Books

AIRLINES SERIES, VOLUME 4

Front cover image: A new Airbus A350 for Turkish Airlines. (Ties Cnossen)

Back cover image: Turkish Airlines joined the Star Alliance as can be seen on this Airbus A330. (Dara Zarbaf, Wikimedia Commons)

Title page image: A Turkish Airlines Boeing 737-800. (Raymond Zammit)

Contents page image: A Turkish Airlines Airbus A321. (Jozef Mols)

Published by Key Books
An imprint of Key Publishing Ltd
PO Box 100
Stamford
Lincs PE19 1XQ

www.keypublishing.com

The right of Jozef Mols to be identified as the author of this book has been asserted in accordance with the Copyright, Designs and Patents Act 1988 Sections 77 and 78.

Copyright © Jozef Mols, 2021

ISBN 978 1 80282 131 4

All rights reserved. Reproduction in whole or in part in any form whatsoever or by any means is strictly prohibited without the prior permission of the Publisher.

Typeset by SJmagic DESIGN SERVICES, India.

Contents

Introduction and Acknowledgements 4
Chapter 1   Devlet Hava Yollari 5
Chapter 2   Post-war Years 13
Chapter 3   Cyprus Turkish Airlines 22
Chapter 4   Liberal Economy 29
Chapter 5   Revamping Turkish Airlines 36
Chapter 6   Into the New Millennium 44
Chapter 7   After Deregulation 49
Chapter 8   Higher Profits Thanks to Deregulation 52
Chapter 9   Biggest in the World 58
Chapter 10   External Factors Play a Key Role 67
Chapter 11   Return to Profitability 72
Chapter 12   A New Era 76
Chapter 13   More Challenges 83
Appendix 1   Incidents and Accidents 88
Appendix 2   Turkish Airlines' Fleet Details 91
Appendix 3   Notes and References 93

Introduction and Acknowledgements

Turkey has always been a bridge between Europe, the Middle East and Asia. The country stands with its legs on both sides of the Bosphorus. To no surprise, different civilisations used this bridge to put their footprint on another continent. In 1200 BCE, the coast of Anatolia was settled by Greeks from the Aeolian and Ionian islands. In the sixth century BCE, the Persian Achaemenid Empire invaded Turkey, resulting in a war between Greek and Persian troops on the coast of Anatolia. In 334 BCE, Alexander the Great came to power, and this would lead to the Hellenization of the region. After his death, Anatolia became part of the Roman Republic. In AD 395, Constantinople would become the capital of the Eastern Roman Empire. Up to that moment, the territory of what is now modern Turkey had mainly been 'invaded' by visitors from either Europe or Central Asia. In later years, the tide would turn when the Ottoman armies started a series of conquests and fought with several European nations over the control of the Mediterranean Sea.

Even today, Turkey still has a 'bridge-function' between Europe on the one hand and the Middle East and Central Asia on the other. This is clearly illustrated by the large number of refugees who flee to Turkey, hoping to enter Europe one day.

With the advent of aviation, this bridge-function would also be used by aviators. When, in 1933, the Turkish government decided to start up a domestic airline (Devlet Hava Yollari/State Airlines Administration), its first pilots were trained in Europe and in the Ottoman Aviation School. The airline started up with a fleet of five aircraft and 24 staff members and would mainly operate domestic flights. This would last until 1956, when Devlet Hava Yollari was restructured and transformed into Turkish Airlines and international ambitions could be realised, mainly after the delivery of the first jets to the airline in 1967. The privatisation of both the Turkish tourism industry and the aviation sector offered new opportunities for Turkish Airlines, despite growing competition in the domestic and international air travel market.

Although Turkish Airlines started out as a domestic airline, it has grown into one of the largest airlines in the world, offering more flight connections than its global competitors at its new Istanbul Airport. Different challenges, such as the devaluations of the Turkish currency, domestic political upheaval, geopolitical factors like the war in neighbouring Syria and the tensions between Turkey and Russia could not stop the airline's growth. Moreover, although the grounding of its Boeing 737-MAX fleet and the COVID-19 pandemic has resulted in new problems, the airline is set on a path of growth that is unique in the aviation industry.

Within this book, I aim to provide some insight into the history of this remarkable airline. Of course, this publication was only possible thanks to the assistance of several people. Therefore, I wish to thank all photographers who allowed me to use their photographs in this book. I also wish to express my gratitude to my partner, Marianne Van Leuvenhaege, for proofreading the manuscript. And, of course, my gratitude also goes to Key for publishing and distributing this book.

Jozef Mols
Wommelgem (Belgium)
15 August 2021

Chapter 1
Devlet Hava Yollari

Aviation in Turkey began even before World War One, when Fesa Evrensev went to France to be trained as a pilot.[1] Evrensev had graduated from the Turkish Military Academy in 1899 as a cavalry lieutenant. In 1911, when the army was looking for someone suitable to become a pilot, he was sent to France to obtain his pilot's licence. When he returned to his hometown in 1912, he was the first Turkish pilot. He participated in the Balkan War and was assigned to the Caucasus Front, but, while trying to reach his place of duty by ship, the Russians sunk the ship and Evrensev was captured near Asmara. Subsequently, he was held as a prisoner in Siberia for nearly six years. He did, however, escape in June 1920.

Evrensev was not the only pioneer of Turkish aviation. Vecihi Hürkuş also played an important role in the start-up. Hürkuş was born in Istanbul in 1896 and participated in the Balkan War as a volunteer. After being injured, he joined the Ottoman Aviation School in Yeşilköy.[2] He made his first solo flight in 1916. After receiving his pilot's licence, he joined the 7th Aircraft Squadron (Tayyare Bölügü) and started bombing and reconnaissance missions against the Russians on the Caucasian Front. During one of these sorties, he shot down a Russian aircraft, becoming the first Turkish pilot to bring down an enemy aircraft. Subsequently, he was taken prisoner by the Russians but managed to escape from Nargin Island, Iran, by swimming. After his return to Istanbul, he joined the 9th Combat Squadron in 1918 and began his mission of protecting Istanbul from attacks from above. During the Turkish War of Independence, he flew as a civilian pilot with the equivalent rank of captain. During this war, he shot down a Greek aircraft. During his service in the war, Hürkuş flew a Russian Caudron G-4, which had been captured by Turkish forces at the Caucasian Front in 1917. A year later, he manufactured a propeller for a captured Russian Nieuport 17. It was clear Hürkuş was not only a good pilot but also an innovative mechanic.[3] Later, he would build several gliders and he would play a key role in the establishment of the Turkish Aeronautical Association. Hürkuş built the Vecihi K-XIV, which was the first civilian aircraft built in Turkey. In 1932, he established a civilian flying school, the Vecihi Sivil Tayyare Mektebi in Kadilkoy. The following year, he trained the first female aviator: Bedriye Tahir Gökmen. Although Hürkuş was never directly involved in the creation of the Turkish flag carrier, he played a major role in the development of commercial aviation in Turkey. On 29 November 1954, he even founded Hürkuş Hava Yollari (Freebird Airlines), the first private airline in Turkey.

On 20 May 1933, Devlet Hava Yollari was established as a domestic airline under the Ministry of Defense with a fleet of 5 aircraft.[4] The initial budget of the organisation was 180,000 Turkish Lira. Fesa Evrensev became its first director. The fleet of Devlet Hava Yollari consisted of two twin-engined Curtiss Kingbirds, two Junkers F13s and a single Tupolev ANT-9. The American Kingbirds were purchased at the price of US$25,555 each and could carry five passengers. They made the first flight of the new airline on 3 February 1933 from Istanbul to Ankara, with a connecting flight to Eskişehir.[5] In the beginning, the Kingbirds were flown by Americans, but they were later replaced by Turkish pilots. The airline started up with 24 staff members, including seven pilots, eight mechanics, eight officers and a radio operator. In 1934, Evrensev was replaced as director by a retired officer by the name of Ayni Bey.

In 1935, the airline was placed under the supervision of the Ministry of Public Works. The budget was increased to 1m Turkish Lira, and Sevket Ari became the general manager. A year later, the airline obtained a de Havilland Dominie (Dragon Rapide) and a Junkers Ju 52 aircraft. Earlier, the airline had used a single de Havilland DH.84 Dragon on loan from the Turkish Air Force. With these additions, the fleet grew to eight aircraft, with a total seating capacity of 64 passengers. From the early days of aviation onwards, Devlet Hava Yollari could count on the support of Kemal Atatürk. He had followed the development of aviation around the world and wanted to take steps to ensure Turkey would not fall behind. In 1937, the airline organised a series of flights over Istanbul in order to promote aviation via the press. A year later, Devlet Hava Yollari was transferred from the Ministry of Public Works to the Ministry of Transportation. Retired pilot Colonel Ferruh Sahinbas started his general manager position, but he would continue to fly for the company as well. By 1939, when the new Güvercinlik Airport in Ankara was opened, the airline could move to a new home. Notwithstanding the fact that large parts of the world were involved in World War Two, the airline managed to purchase six de Havilland Dragon Rapide aircraft, followed by five more Junkers Ju 52s in 1944.

Immediately after World War Two, the airline obtained up to 30 Douglas DC-3s and three Douglas C-47s, several of which were sourced from American air force war surplus in Egypt. This purchase was made possible with the help of Pan American airlines. The American airline also was instrumental in the training of pilots. With this sudden fleet expansion, Devlet Hava Yollari had the largest fleet in the Middle East. The growth of the fleet made it possible to offer domestic flights to 19 destinations. In 1936, another retired military pilot, Colonel Osman Nuri Baykal, became the new general manager.

On 12 February 1947, Devlet Hava Yollari pilots Orhan Ayata and Adil Gözender made the first international flight for the airline. They took off from Ankara on board a DC-3 (TC-ABA) and, after a transfer in Istanbul, flew to Athens. The flight took a total of two hours and 40 minutes. That year, the airline transported, for the first time, around 18,000 passengers. In 1951, the airline – which by now had a fleet of 52 aircraft and a capacity of 845 seats – added Nicosia, Beirut and Cairo to its international route network, but domestic services would remain the airline's focus for many years. The number of passengers more than doubled in 1956 to 37,000.

In 1953, Devlet Hava Yollari decided to start up pilgrimage flights to Jeddah for the large Muslim population of the country. At the same time, a new airport in Istanbul, Yeşilköy, was opened to international air traffic. Its runway was up to international standards, and passengers could enjoy the comfort of a modern terminal. Maintenance hangars and repair shops for radio equipment were also available. Earlier, such maintenance activities had been performed by Turkkusu, established at Güvercinlik Airport. In 1954, Riza Framel became the airline's new general manager. Shortly afterwards, the maintenance facilities of Turkkusu were reorganised under the name of Turkish Technic.

Finally, on 1 March 1956, Devlet Hava Yollari was restructured and transformed into Turkish Airlines (Türk Hava Yollari, THY) as a joint stock company with a capital of 60m Turkish Lira. The same year, Turkish Airlines became a member of IATA, which was established to ensure cooperation in commercial, technical, business and economic areas among its member airlines, as well as to prevent unfair competition.

A monument to Vecihi Hürkuş in Kiziltoprak, Istanbul. (Ceegee, Creative Commons Attribution-Share Alike 4.0 International licence)

A five-seater Curtiss Kingbird, used for mail flights and flown by American pilots. (Jozef Mols collection, photographer unknown, public domain)

A copy of an old black and white negative, which shows a Turkish Curtiss Kingbird. (Jozef Mols collection, photographer unknown, public domain)

Above: A de Havilland Dragon, on loan from the Turkish Air Force. (Turkish Air Force, photographer unknown, public domain)

Right: An old publicity poster, made by Devlet Hava Yollari. (Jozef Mols collection)

Turkish Airlines: The Istanbul Superconnector

The first pilots of Devlet Hava Yollari stand proudly in front of a new de Havilland aircraft. (Jozef Mols collection, photographer unknown, public domain)

A Devlet Hava Yollari aircraft over the Bosphorus. (Turkish Airlines)

Devlet Hava Yollari

A Devlet Hava Yollari aircraft being tanked. (Turkish Airlines)

Pre-flight preparations were rather complex. (Turkish Airlines)

Above: Devlet Hava Yollari obtained some Dakotas shortly after World War Two. (Turkish Airlines)

Left: Cabin crew in front of a Dakota. (Turkish Airlines)

Chapter 2
Post-war Years

During the first years of their existence, Devlet Hava Yollari, and later, Turkish Airlines, were protected from competition by a state monopoly. When Turkey became a member of IATA, it also had to abide by the Chicago Convention, which determined international aviation rules (and still does). However, there was not yet a consensus regarding the trade rights granted under this agreement. Due to this situation, countries around the world needed to contract bilateral and multilateral agreements with each other. Therefore, and in parallel to developing technological and international conditions, the Administration of Civil Aviation (Sivil Havacılık Daire Başkanlığı) was created as a new regulatory body within the Ministry of Transportation, with the aim of protecting national interests. Furthermore, this organisation would be in charge of conducting all international negotiations with regards to the aviation sector and of inspecting the industry on a regular basis. At first, Turkey's membership of IATA did not hamper the development of Turkish Airlines. The airline focused on domestic airline transportation, with the exception of a few routes to nearby locations: flights to Cyprus were started up, as 17 per cent of the Cypriot population were of Turkish origin; flights to Cairo were important, as Egypt had become the political heart of the Middle East since President Nasser had risen to power in 1954; finally, Beirut was an important destination, as it was the financial centre of the Middle East, having hundreds of domestic and international banks and financial institutions.

In 1957, British Overseas Airways Corporation (BOAC) became a partner of Turkish Airlines when the airline took a 6.5 per cent equity share, following the opening up of Turkish Airlines to foreign capital investments.[1] BOAC Director General Sir George Cribbett was appointed as a member of the Board of Directors of Turkish Airlines. Furthermore, the British airline started offering technical assistance. The same year, Turkish Airlines joined SITA (Airlines Worldwide Telecommunications and Information Services) in order to be able to better communicate with airlines around the world.

Fleet modernisation and expansion resulted in the purchase of seven de Havilland Heron aircraft, as well as five Vickers Viscount 794 turboprop aircraft. With this, a new era in the history of Turkish Airlines began, with the switch from piston engines to jet engines. Between 1956 and 1958, the number of passengers carried doubled and reached 394,000. By 1960, at the request of the airline, Turkish Technic started maintenance and revision of Douglas DC-3 aircraft at its Yeşilköy facilities, which had become a modern maintenance centre, and, in this way, started also to get orders from foreign aviation companies. In 1959, an agreement was signed between the maintenance provider and Lockheed International to transform the maintenance centre into a centre able to work for Turkish Airlines, the Turkish Air Force and foreign airlines. At first, 94 Turkish technicians were sent to the US to be trained by Lockheed. Afterwards, a further 62 technicians were trained in-house by Turkish Technic. By 1960, Turkish Technic was able to perform repair and maintenance on nearly 50 per cent of all components of the Douglas Dakota and Vickers Viscount.[2]

In 1959, Turkish Airlines established sales offices in Rome and Athens. The existing Ankara–Istanbul–Athens–Rome route was expanded to Frankfurt in 1960. A year later, a second route from Ankara via Istanbul and Vienna to Frankfurt was opened on a thrice weekly basis. Germany was a very important destination for Turkish Airlines, given the large number of Turkish workers living in Germany. For its domestic routes, the airline obtained six new Fokker F27 aircraft. Two of these aircraft crossed the Atlantic on a 30-hour delivery flight from the US. When looking for an emblem for the airline, Turkish Airlines organised a national competition. Finally, the Wild Goose emblem, designed by Mesut Maniogly, was chosen.

Unfortunately, during this rapid period of expansion, the airline also suffered its first accidents. On 17 February 1959, a Vickers Viscount Type 793 operated a charter flight to London, carrying Turkish Prime Minister Adnan Menderes and a governmental delegation. It was the intention to land at London Heathrow, but, because of weather conditions, the aircraft had to land at London Gatwick instead. The aircraft crashed in dense fog when approaching the airport. Nine of the 16 passengers and five of the eight crew members died. The prime minister, who was seated in the back of the aircraft, survived. Two years later, a Fokker F27-100 crashed at Karanlik Tepe, in the province of Ankara, on approach to Esenboğa Airport. In 1962, a Fairchild (Fokker) F-27 crashed into the Taurus Mountains on approach to Adana Şakirpaşa Airport.

In 1962, veteran Major General Sahap Metel was appointed as the Director General of Turkish Airlines, in line with the tradition of appointing former military officers to this public function.[3] By the time he entered office, Turkish Airlines had a fleet of 34 aircraft with a total seat capacity of 1,120. In 1964, international services to Brussels, Munich and Tel Aviv were launched, and, a year later, the network was further expanded to include Amsterdam, Belgrade and Tabriz. In order to cope with the increasing demand and the expansion of the network, Turkish Airlines leased a series of Douglas DC-7B and DC-7CF cargo aircraft between 1962 and 1968. Some of them were used on scheduled flights to European destinations.

Turkish Airlines entered the jet age when, in 1967, it obtained three McDonnell Douglas DC-9-15 aircraft, one of which (TC-JAA) was leased.[4] Originally, the airline had planned to buy three aircraft of this type, but, because of financial restrictions, it was decided to only buy two aircraft and to lease a third one. The first international jet service started on 1 September 1967, with a flight from Ankara via Istanbul to Brussels. Shortly afterwards, flights to Budapest, Geneva and Zürich were added to the jet route network. By 1968, the capital of the airline had been increased from 90m Turkish Lira to 200m Turkish Lira. All the shares were taken by the Turkish government. By that time, Turkish Technic had upgraded its services to an international standard, and it was able to overhaul most of the components of the fleet, including the new Douglas DC-9 aircraft.

In 1969, two more Douglas DC-9s joined the fleet and Cologne was added to the flight map; a year later, four more Douglas jets were purchased. In Germany, Düsseldorf and Stuttgart routes were put in service. This way, Turkish Airlines was flying to four German cities, providing ample aviation services to the Turkish community there. In the meantime, in 1971, the airline's first Boeing 707 had also been leased, followed by two more a year later. With this, the fleet had grown to 22 aircraft (three Vickers Viscounts, seven Fokker F-27s, eight DC-9-30s, one DC-9-10 and three Boeing 707s) and the total seating capacity had increased to 1,961.

With the purchase of more than 30 Dakotas, Turkish Airlines could start up not only a whole series of domestic routes but also some routes to nearby foreign countries. (Jerry Elmas via Eddie Coates collection)

The Douglas DC-3 would remain the backbone of the Turkish Airlines fleet for many years. (Jerry Elmas via Eddie Coates collection)

De Havilland Heron aircraft were obtained in order to modernise the fleet. (Eddie Coates collection)

In 1958, a total of five Vickers Viscount turboprop aircraft joined the fleet. (Eddie Coates collection)

With the switch from piston to jet engines, a new era in the history of Turkish Airlines began. (Jozef Mols collection)

Fokker F27-100 Friendships started to replace the Dakotas. (Jerry Elmas via Eddie Coates collection)

A postcard edited by the airline showing the Fokker Friendships at the Yeşilköy Airport. (Turkish Airlines)

In 1962, the larger Douglas DC-7 joined the fleet. (Turkish Airlines)

A leased Douglas DC-7 is seen at Brussels International Airport. (Turkish Airlines)

This Viscount crashed in 1959 on approach to London Gatwick. (Jozef Mols collection)

With the introduction of the Douglas DC-9-15, Turkish Airlines entered the jet age. This leased aircraft was named Topkapi and was used on the first jet flight of Turkish Airlines, which linked Turkey with Brussels. (Turkish Airlines)

This Douglas DC-9-32 joined the fleet in 1970 and was sold to Valujet in 1994. (Jozef Mols collection)

Douglas DC-9-15 TC-JAA 'Topkapi' during a promotional press event. (Turkish Airlines)

Turkish Airlines crew in front of a Douglas DC-9 during a press event. (Turkish Airlines)

Boeing 707s allowed the airline to cope with an expanded network and increasing passenger numbers. This Boeing 707-321, designated TC-JBS, was obtained second hand from Pan American in June 1978. (Turkish Airlines)

Boeing 707-300s like TC-JCC were also used in a cargo role. (Turkish Airlines)

With the introduction of the DC-10-30, the seating capacity of the airline was seriously increased. (Turkish Airlines)

Turkish Airlines obtained several Boeing 727-200s. TC-JBH crashed near Isparta, killing all people on board. (Turkish Airlines)

Turkish Airlines: The Istanbul Superconnector

Boeing 727-200 TC-JCK waiting for its passengers. (Turkish Airlines)

Boeing 727-200s were also used by Turkish Cargo. (Turkish Airlines)

Cyprus Turkish Airlines

Turkish-Cypriot carrier Kibris Turkish used some Boeing 727s leased from Turkish Airlines. (Jozef Mols)

The Fokker F28 Fellowship was used on domestic flights. (Turkish Airlines)

Whereas Fokkers served domestic routes, the Douglas DC-9 was used on both domestic and regional routes. (Jozef Mols)

Douglas DC 9-15 TC-JAA, originally operated by Continental Airlines, joined the Turkish Airlines fleet in August 1967. (Turkish Airlines)

Chapter 4
Liberal Economy

In 1980, the multi-party democracy in Turkey was interrupted by a military coup d'état. Prior to the military intervention, the country had known three-digit inflation, a chronic foreign trade deficit and large-scale unemployment.[1] The aim of the military was to unite Turkey with the 'global economy', an aim supported by local business people, giving Turkish companies the ability to market products and services globally. It was hoped that the coup would open the way for greater political stability and might help revitalise the Turkish economy. The regime change would also have a large impact on tourism and the aviation sector.

By the 1960s, development of tourism had spread into Spain and the Italian Adriatic coast, and, by the early 1970s, the former Yugoslavian coast was an emerging holiday region, together with the Greek Islands.[2] Just after the coup, package-based coastal tourism emerged in Turkey, as the government began to regard international tourism as a means of economic development. Incentives for private investment in the sector increased. The Tourism Encouragement Law, adopted in 1982, allocated public land for tourism investment. Whereas, in 1970, some 724,000 tourists visited Turkey, the number increased to over one million by 1980 and to more than four million by 1988.

Prior to 1983, despite a few exceptional cases, only public companies were allowed to do business in the civil aviation industry in Turkey. Turkish Airlines was the only airline for the country, and it dominated the domestic market. Furthermore, all airports were state owned and operated by public companies. After the coup d'état in 1983, the new prime minister, Turgut Ozal, started a reform programme to reduce the state's role in the economy. Turkish Civil Aviation Act No 2920 of 1983 allowed private companies to do business in the civil aviation market. As a result, several private air carriers were set up, becoming direct competition for Turkish Airlines.[3,4] Bursa Airlines was the first private airline to emerge. It started scheduled and unscheduled operations in 1984 but went out of business in 1987. Istanbul Airlines, set up in 1986, managed to survive for 15 years before it went out of business in 2001. The airline was incorporated in 1985 and started its operations on 14 March 1986 with two Sud Aviation Caravelles and two BAC 1-11s, leased from TAROM. In 1987, when the client portfolio was further expanded with more tour operators, two more Caravelles and a Boeing 737-400 were leased, and, later, Boeing 727s replaced the Caravelles. Boğaziçi Hava Taşımacılığı (BHT or Bosphorus Air Transport) was set up in 1987, as a joint venture between Turkish Airlines and private investors. The airline started up freight services with a leased Douglas DC-10-10F and a Boeing 737-321. Additionally, a Boeing 727 was used to fly Turkish workers to and from Germany. However, despite the support of Turkish Airlines, which owned 85 per cent of the shares, the airline went out of business in 1989. Marmara Airlines, set up in 1986, only survived for one year. Other carriers, including Sönmez Airlines, Talia Airlines, Toros Airlines and NESU Airlines, entered the market after the introduction of the new law but were not able to survive competition. Noble Air, set up as a joint venture between British and Turkish investors, concentrated on charter flights to and from London. The airline operated six Boeing 727-200s. In 1990, Noble Air even obtained the rights to fly scheduled services between London and Istanbul, as well as some scheduled domestic routes in Turkey. The airline had to suspend operations in 1991. Toros Air was founded in 1986, with the purpose of transporting

Turkish workers between Ankara and Düsseldorf.[5] The airline started up with a fleet of two leased Boeing 727-200s. After an accident on the ground, the Turkish authorities decided to keep the airline grounded. Turkish workers in Europe constituted the customer portfolio of many of the start-up carriers operating unscheduled flights. As the airlines concentrated on ethnic travel, they could not take a considerable share from the charter market in the first years after the boom of the tourism industry.[6,7] As a result of the increasing competition from private airlines based in Turkey, Turkish Airlines had to make efforts to adapt to the new market situation. In 1983, the airline transported 30,000 tonnes of cargo and 2.5 million passengers on three continents with a fleet of 30 aircraft. The seat capacity had increased to 4,037 and the airline employed 5,775 people. In order to cope with the increased competition, the capital was raised from 20bn Turkish Lira in 1982 to 60bn Turkish Lira in 1984. A year later, four Airbus A310s joined the fleet and flights to the Far East as well as transatlantic flights started. Four de Havilland Canada Dash 7s were also obtained for domestic flights. A first class was introduced, first on routes to Jeddah and London, then followed by other routes. The first flight to the Far East took place in 1986, with the opening of a route to Singapore. New Delhi and Kuala Lumpur followed a year later, as well as a new route to Lyon. With these additions, the number of international passengers exceeded one million, but 2.5 million domestic passengers still formed the backbone of the traffic. Unfortunately, these domestic operations were loss-making, as fares were kept low. These losses were, in part, compensated by transporting workers to and from West Germany and Middle Eastern countries. The addition of three more A310-300s in 1988 enabled the opening of routes to Helsinki, Tunisia, Algeria, Oslo, Basel and New York (via Brussels). In the meantime, the capital had once again been increased, this time to 150bn Turkish Lira in July 1987. In part, as a result of the fleet expansion, and mainly because of high payments for the new Airbus A310s, Turkish Airlines posted losses in 1987 and 1988. Nevertheless, the airline continued to invest in the necessary means to modernise the operations: a baggage handling system was implemented to provide rapid baggage services; two more Airbus aircraft joined the fleet; and the route network was expanding with the introduction of flights to Tokyo, Bangkok and Moscow. Finally, in 1989, seemingly in direct response to the liberalisation of the aviation sector and growing competition, Turkish Airlines and Lufthansa decided to set up a joint venture to establish a new airline. The result, SunExpress, with headquarters in Antalya, would connect Turkish tourism hotspots with several regional airports in Europe. While Turkish Airlines decided to enter the charter market with SunExpress, other private carriers also joined the market. Sultan Air began operations in 1989, using a leased Caravelle 10B, followed by two Boeing 737-200s. However, with the start of the Gulf War, the holiday travel market to Turkey declined. As a result, the airline could only depend upon the transportation of Turkish workers: a sector in which many airlines were competing. Finally, Sultan Air ceased all operations in 1993. Birgenair, founded in 1988, was more successful. It started its operations in August 1989 with a Douglas DC-8-61, which was used initially on special charter flights for Turkish workers. With the growth of mass tourism in Turkey, a close co-operation with a German tour operator allowed the airline to expand. A Boeing 757 joined the fleet in 1992, followed by a Boeing 737-300 a year later. Some of the aircraft were also operated in wet lease for other airlines during the winter months. Following a crash of a Birgenair flight, the airline had to suspend operations in 1996.

With the purchase of Airbus A310s, Turkish Airlines could expand its route network to also cover destinations in Asia. (Jozef Mols collection)

De Havilland Canada Dash 7s joined the domestic fleet and were used for flights to minimally equipped airports. (Turkish Airlines)

Shortly after the liberalisation of the aviation market, Istanbul Airlines started up operations with two Caravelle jets. (Jozef Mols collection)

Istanbul Airlines could rapidly expand, modernise its fleet and became a competitor for Turkish Airlines. (Jozef Mols collection)

Bosphorus European Airlines was another start-up during the months after the liberalisation, but it did not survive. (Jozef Mols collection)

Bogazici Airlines was a joint venture between Turkish private investors and Turkish Airlines. (Jozef Mols collection)

Noble Air was a British–Turkish joint venture, but it did not survive. (Jozef Mols collection)

Birgenair, established as a result of the new liberal aviation policy, was successful in the beginning but lost its licence after the crash of one of its aircraft. (Jozef Mols collection)

Even Sultan Air, also established in the light of the liberal aviation policy, could not survive. (Jozef Mols collection)

SunExpress was a joint venture between Turkish Airlines and Lufthansa, designed to enter the low-cost and holiday market. (Düsseldorf Airport)

Chapter 5

Revamping Turkish Airlines

The second half of the 1980s was – at first glance – not the most prosperous for Turkish Airlines. In both 1987 and 1988, the airline had to post losses. Above all, the liberal approach to aviation by the Turkish government – resulting in the Civil Aviation Act of 1983 – had allowed many private airlines to enter the market. Most of them concentrated on the transportation of Turkish foreign workers, while others offered charter flights for the growing tourism sector. In both cases, their market entrance resulted in competition for Turkish Airlines.

However, there were more challenges to come for Turkish Airlines. In 1987, Turkey applied to join what was then the European Economic Community (EEC).[1] Whereas, on the one hand, such a move would open up the entire European market to Turkish businesses, it would also result in opening up the Turkish aviation market for foreign, primarily European, airlines. Preparing for such possible accession to the EEC would have serious impacts on both the Turkish air transport industry and on the airline management.

Privatisation of the entire aviation sector became a major topic in government circles. Catering company USAS, set up in 1958 by Turkish Airlines, was included among the public enterprises that would be privatised in the first stage of the Privatization Programme, which began in 1980, because it was a profitable monopoly. As a result, all shares of USAS were transferred to the government's Privatization Administration in 1987. In addition, in view of this policy, the ground handling services carried out by USAS were transferred to a new public enterprise, HAVAS Ground Handling Co, which was founded in 1987 and planned to be privatised in the near future. In February 1989, 70 per cent of USAS shares were privatised by block sale to SAS Service Partner, a subsidiary of SAS AB Airlines of Sweden, through an international tender. In October 1993, the remaining shares were sold by the Privatization Administration to the public. Consequently, Turkish Airlines lost its income from its previous majority ownership of USAS.[2]

The airline itself became a target of the Privatization Administration and Turkish Airlines was reclassified as a 'State Economic Enterprise' in 1984, meaning that from now on the government could consider privatising the company. The company was included within the scope of the privatisation by the Council of Ministers on 22 August 1990, and 1.82 per cent of the shares were already privatised through a public offering. Later, in 1994, Turkish Airlines would be placed under the jurisdiction of the Privatization Administration, enabling it to offer shares to private investors whenever the Administration wished.

It is of little surprise then that in order to survive the introduction of liberal aviation laws, the planned privatisation of the airline and Turkey's accession to the EEC, the management of Turkish Airlines saw an urgent need to adapt the management and image of the airline. In March 1990, the airline's capital stock had attained a value of 700bn Turkish Lira, but a year later, this value had increased already to two trillion Lira. In the meantime, the airline had added routes to Benghazi and Budapest and the first Boeing 737s had joined the fleet. In 1992, Turkish Airlines served 69 destinations, including 14 domestic and 55 international. The fleet had been refurbished, both inside and outside, including a new aircraft livery and new uniforms for flight crews and ground staff. Catering services were revamped and improved with multiple-choice menus available on overseas flights. Six Boeing 737-400s and two B737-500s joined the fleet, and routes to Bahrain and Strasbourg began. Between January 1992 and August 1993, the airline also leased an Antonov AN-12 from Air Sofia in order to transport cargo.

By the time Turkish Airlines had been placed under the jurisdiction of the Privatization Administration in 1994, its capital stock value had reached six trillion Turkish Lira. The number of destinations had risen to 78 (23 domestic and 55 international), and, thanks to the aircraft renewal programme, the fleet had an average age of just 6.2 years. Indeed, in July 1993, Airbus A340-300s and Avro RJ-100s began to join the fleet, as well as some extra Boeing 737s. The introduction of the A340 enabled Turkish Airlines to offer direct flights to Tokyo, which were operated with three different classes of service: first, business and economy. In 1994, Turkish Airlines could also start up routes to North American destinations.

BAe jets joined the fleet in the second half of the 1980s. (Jozef Mols collection)

Boeing 737-400s were also part of the fleet renewal in the early 1990s. (Jozef Mols collection)

A Turkish Airlines Boeing 737-400 at Amsterdam's Schiphol Airport. (Jozef Mols)

The new Boeing 737-400s were mainly used on routes to European destinations. (Jozef Mols collection)

The introduction of the Airbus A340 made it possible to offer direct flights from Turkey to Japan. (Jozef Mols collection)

Between January 1992 and August 1993, Turkish Airlines leased this Antonov AN-12 from Air Sofia to complement its cargo fleet. (Jozef Mols collection)

In line with the modernisation of the airline, and to face competition, Turkish Airlines decided to add first-class cabins to its A320-318 fleet in February 1995. Furthermore, during the same year, three Boeing 737-400s, two RJ-100s and a single Airbus A340-300 joined the fleet. This allowed for further expansion of the network with services to Osaka and Tirana and domestic flights to Çanakkale, Bodrum and Tokat. As new passenger aircraft entered the fleet, some older Boeing 727-200s were converted into cargo aircraft and old Douglas DC-9 jets were sold. Notwithstanding the rapid expansion of the airline, staffing levels would be kept at around 8,000 employees, greatly increasing productivity.

In the meantime, SunExpress increased its participation in Cyprus Turkish Airlines. Turkish Airlines, on the other hand, merged with its partially owned domestic subsidiary, THT Inc (Turkish Air Transportation), in September 1993.

Although Turkish Airlines was suffering from the global impact of the Gulf War, its capital continued to rise to ten trillion Turkish Lira in 1995. That year, the company posted for the first time in three years a profit of US$6m on revenues of US$1bn. However, while the airline was profitable again, it had to contend with Turkey's exorbitant inflation of 99.44 per cent in 1995, making any form of capital improvement difficult.[3] The high and persistent inflation had been a major characteristic of the Turkish economy for more than two decades. There were a number of potential causes for the inflation including high public-sector deficits, massive infrastructure investments, high military expenditures, political instability and changes in exchange rates on imported goods, among others.

In 1996, the Turkish government decided to deregulate the domestic air transportation market, enabling new scheduled competition from charter airlines.[4] At the same time, larger international carriers were providing stiff competition on routes to Western Europe. In order to increase its market share, the airline launched its own website, and the route network was further expanded to include Tbilisi, Sarajevo and Johannesburg and domestic flights to Konya, Sinop and Kahramanmaraş. At the same time, Turkish Airlines fully understood it would not be possible to tackle competition on its own, so the airline started looking for different forms of cooperation. In 1997, a 'block space' agreement was signed with Japan Airlines on the Istanbul–Osaka–Istanbul route. Other jointly operated flights would follow soon, and Turkish Airlines joined Austrian Airlines, Swissair and Croatian Airlines under the umbrella of the Qualiflyer Group. To further modernise its fleet of passenger jets, six Boeing 737-800 aircraft would be delivered to Turkish Airlines in 1998. A year later, another nine 737-800s and one Airbus A340-300 were received. With this, the fleet consisted of 75 aircraft, carrying 10.6 million passengers per year. Just before the end of the millennium, a new codeshare agreement was signed with Malaysia Airlines for the Istanbul–Kuala Lumpur–Istanbul route.

At the same time cargo operations were growing, Turkey's manufacturing sector was also taking off.[5] As Turkey is situated on the ancient trade routes of the Silk Road, the country had strong links with both several former Soviet republics, such as Turkmenistan, Kazakhstan, and Uzbekistan, and with some Middle Eastern countries, facilitating easy trade agreements. According to *Air Cargo World*, Turkish Airlines held a 40 per cent share of Turkey's international cargo market, with most business coming from Germany, with its large expatriate Turkish population.[6] Cargo was accounting then for about US$5m of Turkish Airlines' annual revenues. By the end of the 1990s, the company had a registered capital of 175 trillion Turkish Lira. Its fleet consisted primarily of Airbus A310s and A340s and Boeing 737s. In order to maintain the fleet, a second maintenance base hangar with a 13,000m² closed area was opened at Atatürk Airport in 1999. This enabled the airline to organise maintenance and repair services through Turkish Technic for its entire fleet, as well as for other airlines.

Despite these developments, the end of the millennium was not all that positive for Turkish Airlines, and it had to announce a loss of US$167m in 1999; this was primarily the result of terrorist threats and an earthquake in northwest Turkey, which resulted in the deaths of more than 17,000 people. More than half a million people were left homeless, and, of course, tourism to Turkey suffered from this catastrophe.

The airline merged with its partially owned domestic subsidiary, THT Inc. (Jozef Mols collection)

New Boeing 737-800s joined the fleet in 1999. (Jozef Mols collection)

By the end of the millennium, Turkish Airlines' Boeing 737-800s could be seen at most European airports. (Jozef Mols collection)

To maintain its growing fleet, Turkish Airlines had to train a lot of technicians for its maintenance base. (Turkish Airlines)

This Boeing 777-300ER joined the Turkish Airlines fleet in August 2011. (Jozef Mols collection)

Chapter 6
Into the New Millennium

The 'new millennium' was considered to be a significant milestone by many, presenting new possibilities for companies around the globe. However, of course, it was only just 'more of the same', as the changing of a date does not mean that much. That was also true for Turkish Airlines, which continued on the path of expansion, larger market share and profitability... but also continued to encounter many challenges.

The year 2000 saw the arrival of seven Boeing 737-800 aircraft, as well as a new Airbus A340-300. Whereas, on the one hand, the codeshare agreement with Austrian Airlines expired, new contracts were signed regarding long-haul flights. The airline agreed upon a block space arrangement on the Istanbul–Seoul–Istanbul route with Asiana Airlines. American Airlines signed a codeshare agreement regarding domestic connections between New York, Miami and Chicago and ten domestic destinations in American's network. Consequently, Turkish Airlines was able to offer a total of 13 destinations in the US from Istanbul, as its transatlantic flights connected seamlessly to American's domestic routes. With Cathay Pacific Airlines, a block space agreement was signed on the Istanbul–Hong Kong–Istanbul route. Turkish Airlines also opened a route to Sydney to enable European passengers to visit the 2000 Sydney Olympic Games. Within Europe, codeshare agreements were signed with LOT Polish Airlines on the Istanbul–Warsaw–Istanbul route, and with CSA Czech Airlines, covering the Istanbul–Prague–Istanbul route. Notwithstanding its ambitions to be present on all continents, either through flights operated by itself or by third parties via commercial agreements, Turkish Airlines withdrew from the Swissair-led Qualiflyer alliance. This decision should be seen as a means of attracting as many strategic investors as possible for the further privatisation of the airline, planned for later.

All the new agreements made it possible for Turkish Airlines to offer more destinations, and thus extend its international reach, without having to increase its fleet size. The purchase or leasing of new aircraft should rather be seen as a modernisation of the fleet. When, in 2001, two more Boeing 737-800s joined the fleet, six older Airbus A310-200s were sold to Iran Air. The same year, Turkish Airlines signed a codeshare agreement with SunExpress, in which it participated as a shareholder, covering the Antalya–Frankfurt–Antalya route; the Turkish coast had become a tourist hotspot, especially in the German market.

Expansion was hampered by the economic crisis in Turkey in 2001, which mainly cut traffic on domestic routes. Additionally, further liberal aviation policies enacted by the government took their effect. Prior to 2001, Turkish Airlines and other private airlines were not allowed to determine their ticket prices for domestic flights, since the Turkish Civil Aviation Act of 1983 had not guaranteed such freedom.[1] However, the amendments to the act, made on 26 April 2001, gave airlines the right to freely determine their fares for domestic routes. Thus, the amendment allowed for price setting based upon commercial considerations in the marketplace. Furthermore, the Act of 1983 had not fully opened the domestic market to private carriers, still giving Turkish Airlines a limited protection from competition. However, a new amendment, voted on in 2003, would allow such competition in domestic flights and remove barriers that inhibited private airline companies from entering the market. Furthermore, the government also lifted some additional taxes on domestic air transport and reduced airport service charges in airports, which were run by the General Directorate of State Airports. The costs to airlines were thus reduced, and this reduction was reflected in ticket prices.

Following the liberalisation of price tariffs in 2001, the domestic market had become completely open, which paved the way for significant changes. As a direct result of this reduction, there was a considerable increase in the number of passengers carried on domestic flights; between 2003 and 2006, the number of domestic passengers increased by 191 per cent. Although this increase can be attributed primarily to the cost reduction, the increase in frequency on existing routes was an important factor as well. In addition, the new entrant airlines operated flights on new routes to which Turkish Airlines had never flown. Turkish Airlines would – for the first time in its existence – have to face competition from low-cost airlines. Onur Air, which was a charter airline before 2003, became one of the first carriers to introduce domestic scheduled airline transportation after the deregulation. Onur Air targeted middle-income level customers and developed a strategy of offering low fares with low cost and low profit margins, addressing the needs of an extended group of customers.

Following the 11 September 2001 terrorist attacks on the US, Turkish Airlines also managed to survive the downturn in air travel without a government bailout or mass layoffs. Nevertheless, 300 middle management positions were eliminated; 400 part-timers were laid off and wages were cut by 10 per cent. According to *Turkish Daily News*, the airline's survival was the result of entrepreneurial management and the ability to cancel loss-making routes at home and abroad. Despite these problems, and merely a year later, in 2002, another two Boeing 737-800s entered service. On 18 September 2003, Turkish Airlines started flying to New Delhi. A codeshare agreement with Air India was signed two months later, covering the joint operation of the Istanbul–New Delhi–Istanbul route. However, once again, external factors would influence the results of Turkish Airlines and the global airline industry. The war in Iraq in 2003 prompted Turkish Airlines to close some routes in the Persian Gulf, and flights to Asia were suspended during the SARS epidemic.[2] However, the airline would soon recover.

In 2004, Turkish Airlines transported 12 million passengers. Of course, expansion requires training of cockpit crews, cabin crews and ground staff. In order to answer the needs of the airline, the Turkish Airlines Flight Academy was established at the Aydın airport. Courses offered include ATP (Unified Airline Transport Pilot Training), Private Pilot Licence, Modular Instrument Flight Rating, Modular Airline Transport Pilot Theoretical Knowledge Course, Commercial Pilot Licence and Instrument Flight Rating Course, Instructor Training and MCC training. The school had a maximum capacity of 200 students per year, and courses were organised by 34 instructors. Residential accommodations were available at Golf Resort Hotel and the costs were covered by the flying school. For starters, the school ordered a series of Cessna 172S NAV III Skyhawk aircraft.

Turkish Airlines' faith in the future was best underlined by a massive order in 2004. The airline announced the order of 36 jets from Airbus, worth US$2.8bn, as well as another 15 Boeing 737s. The Airbus order included A330-200, A321-200 and A320-200 aircraft. With these new aircraft, the airline planned to open 23 new international routes. However, Turkish Airlines was not just opening new routes and ordering new aircraft, it was also planning to spend US$350m on a new technical and training facility at Istanbul's underutilised Sabiha Gökçen International Airport. At that time, Turkish Technic was employing 2,700 people and was planning to hire another 2,000 by 2010. The flying school also received three flight simulators.

Whereas almost all airports in Turkey were public-owned companies and run by the State Airports Authority, the Sabiha Gökçen Airport – founded in January 2001 – was the second largest airport in

Istanbul, and it was not run by the State Airports Authority.[3] The airport did not manage to unburden the traffic of Atatürk Airport, which airlines preferred, and thus it remained almost inactive until the end of 2004. Nevertheless, with the re-deregulation of domestic flights, the passenger and aircraft traffic on domestic routes had begun to accelerate rapidly. As a result, slot problems emerged for domestic flights, particularly at Atatürk Airport, and Turkish Airlines decided to move some domestic flights to the Sabiha Gökçen Airport as of April 2005. Ground handling and airport service charges are lower at this airport, resulting in lower ticket prices.

In 2004, Turkish Airlines' shares were publicly traded, but the government still owned 98 per cent. The privatisation programme was revived with a public offering of 20 per cent of the shares on the Istanbul Stock Exchange.[4] After the offering, the government would still own 75 per cent of the shares. The offering itself would raise US$170m. At the same time, the airline was divesting its 50 per cent holding in Cyprus Turkish Airlines, a deal which was concluded in 2005. Although Turkish Airlines had to face the entry of new competitors into the market, the future looked bright and tourism was booming, with 20 million people expected to visit the country in 2005, versus 12 million in 2003. However, in 2005, a significant change would come to bookkeeping, as New Turkish Lira replaced Old Turkish Lira, with one of the former being the equivalent of one million of that latter.

In the first year of the new millennium, Turkish Airlines received seven new Boeing 737-800s. (Raymond Zammit)

The Flying Academy uses a fleet of Cessna 172 aircraft. (Turkish Airlines)

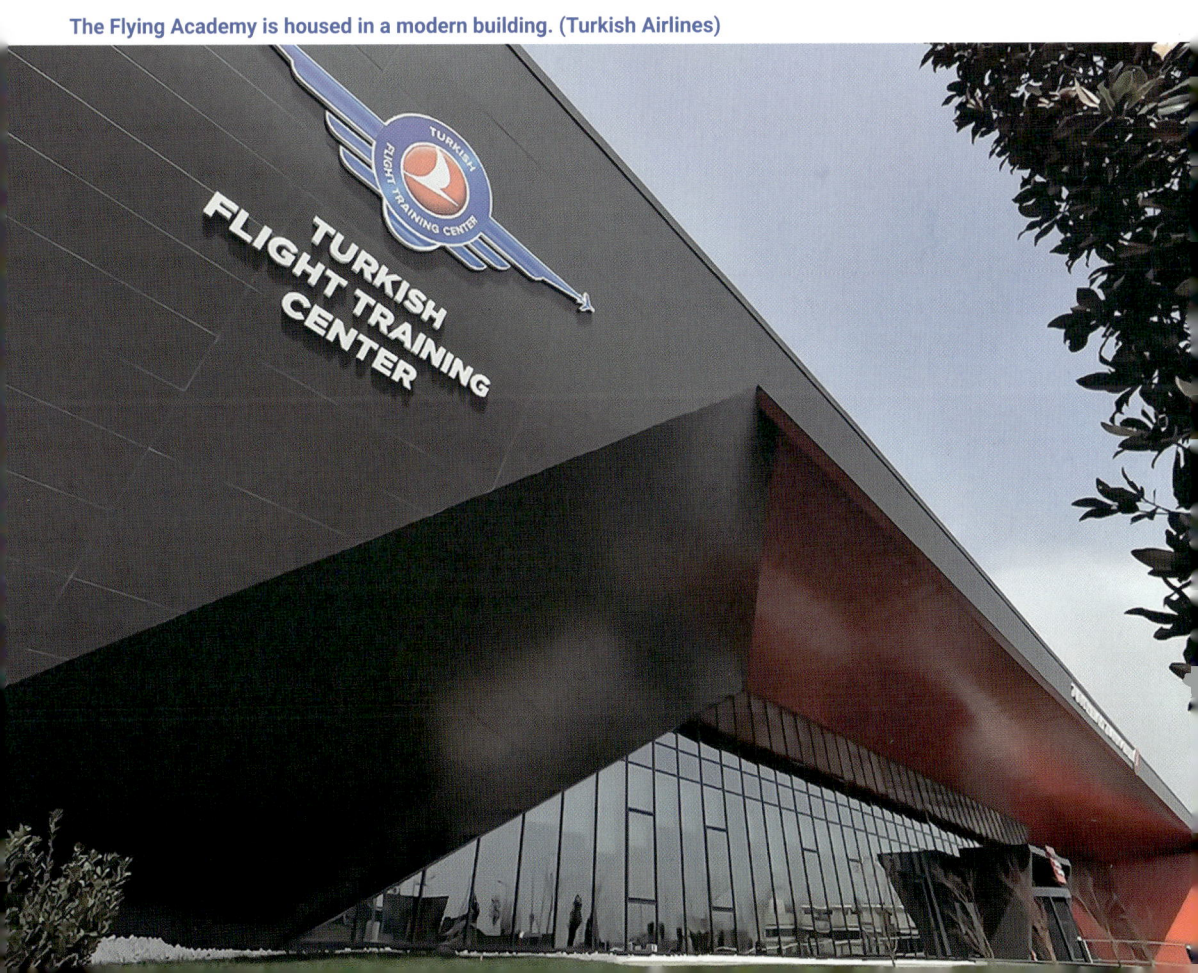

The Flying Academy is housed in a modern building. (Turkish Airlines)

A series of flight simulators is used for the training of future Turkish Airlines pilots. (Turkish Airlines)

An Airbus A 330-200F of Turkish Cargo. (Alec Wilson on Wikimedia Commons)

Chapter 7
After Deregulation

The deregulation of Turkish aviation was probably the most important, and also the most complex, event in the country's aviation history. The actual deregulation came into force in 2003, when the barriers to market entry were removed, providing the primary condition for competition.[1] After 2003, the domestic market had broken away from the monopolistic structure and was converted into a market with multiple numbers of airlines. However, it would take a while before players in the market could fully respond to the new rules governing their activities. Onur Air started up domestic flights in December 2003, shortly after the deregulation came into effect, Atlas Jet entered the market in July 2004, and Pegasus Air would start its domestic flights in November 2005. Obviously, Turkish Airlines had less to adapt to, considering it has been in the airline transportation business for a longer period of time, and this, of course, resulted in a competitive advantage.

Although, in theory, all barriers to market entry had been removed along with deregulation, some barriers still existed – the most significant being the lack of sufficient capacity at Atatürk Airport.[2] As previously stated, some airlines that entered the domestic market therefore selected to operate from the Sabiha Gökçen International Airport. As a result, two different markets were created; if one considers that nearly a quarter of the Turkish population is located in Istanbul and its environs, and that there is a long distance between Atatürk International and Sabiha Gökçen – even if the starting point is Istanbul – it is inevitable that these two airports will create different markets.

Turkish Airlines may have had a competitive advantage over the new entrants in the domestic market, but it still had to adapt to the new market conditions. As ticket prices came down, the airline had to reduce costs. Turkish Airlines was seen as the price maker in the market, and Onur Air tried to offer lower prices, as did the other new entrants.[3] The competition between airlines would – in the long term – lead to the implementation of yield management and a dynamic pricing system. However, although Turkish Airlines was forced to develop cost reduction strategies, it did not want to do so to the detriment of service quality. In other words, cost reduction strategies were implemented, not by abolishing services passengers could experience, but by a series of changes in the management processes. As part of the efficient fleet planning process, aircraft were purchased when the world economy was suffering crisis, and thus at a lower price. The purchase of Airbus 320 and Boeing 737 jets can be seen in this light. Daily utilisation rates were increased, and more productive operations were ensured. Though the fleet grew, resources, excluding the cabin and cockpit crew, were kept stable so that there was no significant increase in costs. Eventually, through all these measures, production on a passenger-mileage basis increased, costs were unchanged, and productivity was improved. As an increase in production requires a high-volume service purchase from suppliers, this reinforced Turkish Airlines' bargaining power.

Another major response to deregulation was the development of outsourcing strategies. Turkish Airlines wanted to concentrate on its core competences and gave up producing subsidiary services. Technical services, catering services, ground handling and call centres were all converted into stand-alone administrations with their own company identity and commercial activities. Additionally, these companies could provide services to third parties and generate income and reduce their unit costs thanks to their economies of scale. The establishment of THY Habom AS, THY Teknik AS and

THY Egitim in November 2005 are good examples of this strategy. THY Habom would provide aircraft maintenance services like airframe maintenance, modification and overhaul services, component repairs, paint services and engineering support for a variety of commercial, business and leasing companies. THY Teknik was set up as a stand-alone maintenance centre, taking over the activities of the previous maintenance organisation, and THY Egitim became the stand-alone flying school. However, the outsourcing did not result in staff reduction. On 31 December 2005, Turkish Airlines employed 11,121 people, compared to 10,956 a year before.

On 15 December 2005, the first three aircraft of the Airbus and Boeing orders joined the fleet. They included a 737-800, an A320 and Turkey's first A330. The same year, a new pricing model had been put into effect, benefitting customers. Also in 2005, new routes were opened to Casablanca, Lisbon, Oslo and Astana. In June 2005, flights linking Istanbul and Antalya with London's Stansted Airport were also introduced. A year later, in 2006, the network was further expanded to include Ljubljana, Abu Dhabi, Dushanbe, Rostov, Donetsk, Tabriz, Kazan, Belgrade, St Petersburg, Helsinki, Muscat, Venice, Dublin, Riga, Addis Ababa, Yekaterinburg, Dnipropetrovsk, Mumbai, Minsk, Osaka, Lagos, Singapore and Nairobi. The link with Kenya was a direct result of an agreement with Kenya Airways. As Turkish Airlines was expanding its route map, the fleet had also grown. In 2006, its 100th aircraft joined the fleet. There is no doubt that Turkish Airlines had proven to be able to grow while maintaining outstanding service levels. In 2006, the airline was invited to become a member of the Star Alliance; full membership would follow in 2008, when Turkish Airlines would become the seventh European airline to join the alliance and the twentieth member of the network. In order to further increase service levels, a new service was launched on 18 August 2006, allowing passengers without luggage to check in and print their boarding cards using the internet.

It became clear that measures taken to tackle competition after deregulation would also have other widespread consequences. As Turkish Airlines tried to compete by offering high standards of service, its Star Ranking status was upgraded from 3-Star to 4-Star Quality Certified Airline. In the meantime, Turkish Airlines had also obtained the ISO 9001:2000 quality certificate. As a result of the excellent performance of the airline, the government decided the time was ripe for a further privatisation of the company. In May 2006, 25 per cent of the shares in Turkish Airlines were sold through a public offering. After this second round of offerings, the government participation in Turkish Airlines was reduced to 46.46 per cent. The shares were traded on the Istanbul Stock Exchange as of 25 May 2006, but soon they fell below their public offering price. Hereupon, the Privatisation Authority had to purchase shares for 30 days in order to ensure price stability. As a result, the participation of the State increased again to 49.12 per cent. As the state-owned share of Turkish Airlines had fallen below 50 per cent, the airline was no longer considered a public-owned enterprise in legal terms, and it became a joint stock company under Turkish commercial law. This was a very important development, as the management of the airline gained considerable flexibility, particularly in purchases. As shares in Turkish Airlines were free-float shares, it meant that shareholders holding 2 per cent or more of shares were entitled to nominate candidates for membership of the executive board, and these candidates did not have to bear Turkish citizenship.[4] Nevertheless, the influence of political groups continued in the administration, and although foreigners could now obtain shares in Turkish Airlines via the stock exchange, the share of control was not sold to a strategic investor.

The first A320s arrived by the end of 2005. (Alf Van Beem, Wikimedia Commons, public domain)

By the end of 2005, the first Airbus A330 jets joined the fleet. (Lukas von Daeniken, Wikimedia Commons)

participate.[8, 9] According to Sidney Dekker, who carried out a study about the human factors in air crashes, it was clear that Boeing and the FAA tried to blame the Turkish Airlines pilots for the crash, so they did not have to mention the construction errors in the Boeing 737 NG.[10] According to Dekker, Boeing was already aware five years before the crash that faulty sensors could command the autopilot to throttle down and thus reduce speed. Although Boeing had offered a software solution for this problem, this solution could not be installed on older aircraft of the same type… and the crashed aircraft was such an older aircraft. Dekker's report was, however, removed from the official investigation papers. According to Dekker, knowledge of these construction errors could have made a difference when building the Boeing 737 MAX later on. This was not the only criticism regarding the accident. According to surviving passengers, it took a long time after the crash for the rescue teams to arrive. Following media speculation, a spokesperson for the prosecutor's office in Haarlem confirmed in April 2009 to *Agence France-Presse* that instructions were given following the crash to remove four laptops from the wreckage prior to the start of rescue operations.[11] These laptops were to be handed over to the American embassy in The Hague. According to the Dutch newspaper *De Telegraaf*, some Boeing employees aboard the crashed flight were in possession of laptops with confidential military information. According to Turkish media outlets *Radikal* and *Sozcu*, the Boeing employees on board were in possession of confidential military information and the rescue response was delayed because American officials had specifically requested from the Dutch authorities that no one was to approach the wreckage until the confidential information was retrieved. According to *Radikal*, the then CEO of Turkish Airlines, Temel Kotil, had also stated that a Turkish Airlines employee, stationed at Schiphol Airport, had arrived at the crash site with his apron-access airport identification badge but was prevented from reaching the wreckage and was handcuffed and detained by Dutch police after resisting.[12] While the *De Telegraaf* article and some Turkish sources alleged that FBI and CIA agents were on site for recovery, this was denied by the prosecutor's office. However, one fact remains certain: one of the cockpit crew members was still alive when the accident response team arrived at the crash site, but, because of delays in the rescue operations, he died before his body could be removed from the wreckage.[13]

Fortunately, although the accident was a big shock for Turkish Airlines, it did not hamper its further ambitions. Past results indeed encouraged the management of the airline; operating profits had increased from 722,759,224 New Turkish Lira in 2007 to 723,890,442 in 2009. In 2010, the airline had transported 47,949,909 revenue passengers, and its load factor had increased from 70.9 per cent in 2009 to 73.7 per cent in 2010. In 2011, the expansion continued with the addition of Guangzhou, Shiraz, Valencia, Erbil, Toulouse, Malaga, Genoa, Basra, Thessaloniki, Naples, Al Najaf, Kabul, Sulaymaniyah, Islamabad and Turin on the route map.

On 13 June 2001, Turkish Airlines joined Arab Air Carriers Organization (AACO) as partner airline of the regional airline association. While preparing for its partner airline membership, the airline developed bilateral links with a number of AACO-established partners. Turkish Airlines had already operated codeshare flights with Egyptair, Etihad Airways, Royal Air Maroc and Syrian Arab Airlines. According to Mr Abdul Wahab Teffha, the then secretary general of AACO, the membership of Turkish Airlines was fully in line with the history of the region. The Arab region and Turkey have been coupled by geography and by human relations for millennia, and it was only natural that cooperation between Arab airlines and Turkish Airlines continued to flourish. In June 2011, Turkish Airlines had already received three *Skytrax* nominations for 'Best Airline Europe', 'Best Airline Southern Europe' and 'Best Premium Economy Seats'.

In order to face competition, SunExpress – which is 50 per cent owned by Turkish Airlines – started up a hub at the Sabiha Gökçen Airport in Istanbul. (Düsseldorf Airport)

After the deregulation of aviation in Turkey, Pegasus became the major competitor of Turkish Airlines. (Jozef Mols collection)

AnadalouJet became a second brand of Turkish Airlines and was set up to operate flights from Ankara Airport to cities in Anatolia. (Jozef Mols collection)

Turkish Airlines became an important member of the Star Alliance Group. (Jozef Mols collection)

The crash of a Boeing 737-800 in Amsterdam was a warning for later accidents for 737 MAX aircraft, but Boeing did not heed the necessary lessons. (Radio Nederland Wereldomroep, Wikimedia Commons)

Turkish Airlines bought two Cessna Mustangs for its training school. (Raymond Zammit)

Chapter 9

Biggest in the World

Expansion does not come without a price, and that is also true for Turkish Airlines. In 2011, operating profits dropped from 482,188,606 New Turkish Lira in 2010 to 191,088,816 New Turkish Lira. Sales costs were especially responsible for this evolution, as they increased by nearly 50 per cent because of expensive marketing efforts. The expansion of the route map also had some impact. Although the airline had carried 18,160,193 passengers (up from 15,474,133 in 2010), the load factor on the expanded route network had decreased from 73.1 per cent to 71.9 per cent. Besides this, Turkish Airlines had also signed an expensive sponsorship deal with Manchester United, replacing Air Asia as the team's official carrier. At the time of the sponsorship, the football team's debts had risen to £716m, but the accounts of Manchester United's parent group, Red Football Joint Venture, showed that the club's sponsorship income had grown 48 per cent! In 2010, Turkish Airlines had already signed a sponsorship deal with Euroleague Basketball and had become the major sponsor of Eurocup, the biggest basketball competition in Europe. The same year, Turkish Airlines also sponsored football club Barcelona. Under the deal, Turkish Airlines would transport the players of Barcelona to all the tournaments and training camps.

In 2011 and 2012, a total of seven Airbus A319-100 aircraft had joined the fleet. In 2012, Turkish Airlines secured the number one spot (according to the *Official Airline Guide*) in terms of the number of countries it flies to.[1] The airline now had 90 countries around the globe on its route map, more than any other airline in the world. The same year, the airline also reached another milestone, adding its 200th aircraft; the Boeing 737-900 – the airline's ninth – was the newest addition to the fleet. The aircraft was adorned with a special '200' sticker.

In 2012, Turkish Airlines announced a sponsorship deal with Ligue 1 giant Olympique de Marseille, to become the official airline of the French club for the 2013–14 season.[2] This deal offered the airline the opportunity to promote its recently established route from Istanbul to Marseille.

A year later, in 2013, Turkish Airlines once again entered into sponsorship deals with sports clubs. When the airline replaced its 'Globally Yours' motto, which had been accompanying the airline for years, with the 'Widen Your World – Explore the World Bigger' motto, a new commercial was made, starring Kobe Bryant and Lionel Messi in different parts of the world. On 2 May 2013, Turkish Airlines announced an agreement with Borussia Dortmund, champion in both the 2010 and 2011 seasons for the German football league, Bundesliga.[3] This way, Turkish Airlines became the airline of choice for all Borussia Dortmund international flights. The same year, Turkish Airlines also signed a similar sponsorship deal with Aston Villa, one of the long-established football clubs in England. Also in 2013, Turkish Airlines hosted 48 million passengers on its aircraft, and became Europe's number two airline in terms of passenger loads. By the end of the year, Turkish Airlines could proudly announce it had carried more than 48 million passengers, and its load factor had gone up to 79 per cent.

Fleet expansion and fleet modernisation remained important for Turkish Airlines. In 2013, it became known that the airline had signed a contract for up to 117 Airbus A320 Family aircraft (78 A321neos, four A320neos and options for 35 additional A321neo aircraft). This order was the largest order ever placed by a Turkish carrier. At the time of the order, Turkish Airlines was already operating 75 A320 Family aircraft. The new order was to help Turkish Airlines expand its short- and medium-haul routes from its Istanbul hub, while the aircraft's commonality with its existing Airbus fleet would generate additional cost savings.[4] Incorporating new engines and large Sharklet wing tip devices, the A320neo Family would deliver fuel savings of 15 per cent and they would result in a double-digit reduction in NOx emissions. At the same time as the Airbus deal, Turkish Airlines also ordered 95 aircraft from Boeing (20 737-800s, 65 737-8 MAXs and ten 739-9 MAXs) all to be delivered until 2021.

In 2014, Turkish Airlines took different measures to make travel even more enjoyable. Sky Illusion sleep sets were introduced on long-haul flights, including beauty products and Aloe Vera extracts. Furthermore, new seats, created and built by a partnership between Turkish Airlines, Turkish Seats Industries and Turkish Technic were installed on Boeing 737-800 aircraft, and later also on the A319s, A320s and A321s. As Istanbul became a major hub, and Turkish Airlines was offering long-distance flights via this hub with passengers originating from all parts of the world, the airline decided time in transit should be more enjoyable. Therefore, they introduced the Touristanbul Service, enabling passengers with several hours of transit time to visit the highlights of Istanbul before boarding their connecting flight. As a result of all efforts, the airline was once again awarded the 'Best Airline in Europe' award at the *Skytrax* Passenger's Choice Awards. Service levels were further enhanced in 2015 with the opening of an Arabic call centre, which served ten countries in the Middle East. And, of course, the sponsorship marketing policy was extended. Turkish Airlines achieved a first in the 55-year history of the European Football Championship when it signed a sponsorship agreement with UEFA as the 'first official airline sponsor' of the UEFA 2016, which took place in France.[5] The Bundesliga club Hannover 96 was also sponsored by the airline, and it became the official partner of the European Rugby Champions Cup and the Challenge Cup. Turkish Airlines also wanted to sponsor the cultural sector, so it became the official sponsor of the International Antalya Golden Orange Film Festival. Because of all efforts by the airline management, the brand value of the airline – which stood at US$1.6bn in 2012 – reached US$2.2bn in 2015. No wonder Turkish Airlines' Investor Relations were chosen as the 'Best Investor Relations in Turkey' in 2015 by the *IR Magazine*. Needless to say, the airline was once again heavily awarded by *Skytrax*, winning 'Best Business Class Lounge Dining' (2014 and 2015), 'Best Business Class Airline Catering' (2013–15) and 'Best Airline in Europe' (five times in a row, 2011–15). Above all, *anna.aero* discovered Istanbul had become the best-connected airline hub by region thanks to Turkish Airlines' network.

There are many ways to compare airline hubs, but Istanbul is connected to the most hubs in terms of total number of destinations served non-stop. However, this does not take into account the frequency of services nor the aircraft size.[6] Regardless, Turkish Airlines overtook Delta Airlines in Atlanta for the claim of having the biggest single-hub network of non-stop destinations. In 2015, Turkish Airlines was flying to 235 international destinations in 113 countries. The airline had carried more than 61 million passengers, up from 55 million in 2014. If one looks at the regional breakdown, North America was Turkish Airlines' most important destination, accounting for 20.5 per cent of all passengers, followed by South America (13.7 per cent) and the Far East (13.5 per cent). Passengers flying to the Middle East accounted for some 11.4 per cent, whereas traffic to European destinations accounted for 8.5 per cent. Domestic traffic (16 million passengers) was good for 16.1 per cent. In 2015, the airline made an operating profit of 2,995m New Turkish Lira, up from 1,443m the previous year. No wonder politicians in Turkey started to think about building a new, bigger, airport.

In order to fulfil its functions as the best-connected airline, Turkish Airlines had to further expand its fleet. In 2015, the airline firmed up a commitment for the purchase of 20 additional A321neo aircraft. In the meantime, six Embraer E190/E195 aircraft had also joined the fleet, bringing the total to 299 aircraft, of which ten were cargo aircraft. This fleet expansion programme was fully in line with the '2008–2023 Fleet Projection Program'.

In 2011 and 2012, a total of seven Airbus A319-100 aircraft jointed the fleet. (Raymond Zammit)

Turkish Airlines became the sponsor of Manchester United. (Wadman, Wikimedia Commons)

Turkish Airlines sponsored FIBA Basketball World Cup. (Ercan Karakas, Wikimedia Commons)

Turkish Airlines also sponsored EuroLeague Basketball. (Nuerenberg Airport)

Above: Another shot of the Manchester United livery for Turkish Airlines. (Turkish Airlines)

Left: Of course, the sponsorship of football club Barcelona, one of the first of such deals by Turkish Airlines, was used for major publicity. (Turkish Airlines)

Biggest in the World

The airline also sponsored Borussia Dortmund. (Jozef Mols collection)

In 2012, Turkish Airlines added the 200th aircraft to its fleet. (Turkish Airlines)

In 2013, Turkish Airlines took delivery of several Airbus A321s, including TC-JSI, under the '2008–2023 Fleet Projection Program'. (Raymond Zammit)

Airbus A321 TC-JSJ was also delivered in 2013 and painted in the colors of Borussia Dortmund. (Raymond Zammit)

Some earlier A320s were repainted in a retro colour scheme. (Jozef Mols collection)

While waiting delivery of its own Airbus aircraft, Turkish Airlines frequently leased equipment from other airlines, like this Airbus A320. (Jozef Mols)

For a very short period of time in the early 2000s, Turkish Airlines used a Bell 430 helicopter for VIP flights. (Jozef Mols collection)

When Turkish Airlines sponsored the UEFA football competition in France, an Airbus had to be repainted with the logos of the event. (Jozef Mols collection)

Chapter 10
External Factors Play a Key Role

The early years of the 21st century had seen Turkish Airlines achieve optimum results, and 2016 also started out well. The company received the 'Low Carbon Hero' award, as it succeeded in keeping its carbon consumption at a low level. With the 'Fuel Savings Program', initiated in 2008, the airline implemented more than 100 operational optimisation projects that would reduce its carbon footprint. With these applications, fuel consumption had been reduced by 572,000 tons in the last 5 years, and its flights had become 20 per cent more efficient than five years earlier.

In March 2016, Turkish Airlines had announced its partnership with Warner Bros Pictures on the highly anticipated action-adventure film *Batman versus Superman: Dawn of Justice*. In the movie, a pivotal scene unfolds aboard a Turkish Airlines-owned Boeing 777. Of course, the airline used this opportunity to offer its fans innovative movie-themed experiences, which gave the fans an inside look at the world of the iconic superheroes.[1] The same year, the airline was supposed to take delivery of six Boeing 777-300ERs and 20 737-800NGs (some of which were delivered on time, and some of which came later), bringing the fleet size at over 310 aircraft. Turkish Airlines was targeting 72 million passengers in 2016, compared to 61.2 million in 2015.

Notwithstanding all this good news, the first quarter of 2016 did not end on a positive note for the airline. Turkish Airlines had to announce an operating loss of 630m Turkish Lira for the first three months of the year, compared to an operating profit of 42m Turkish Lira over the same period a year earlier. The airline had carried 14.2 million passengers on 108,000 flights with an average load factor of 74 per cent during this first quarter. The number of transfer passengers had increased by 22 per cent. However, intense domestic and international competition had put pressure on ticket prices. And the worst was still to come.

Airlines are not only influenced by macro-economic factors. In most countries, politics also play an important role, and this is also the case in Turkey. Turkey had undergone significant transformations since the Justice and Development Party (AKP) came to power in 2002, which was illustrated by the growth of the airline industry. Turkish Airlines clearly benefitted from the support of the national authorities, who considered the carrier to be a strategic instrument in consolidating Turkey's influence internationally and in building solid cooperation with foreign states.[2] The expansion of Turkish Airlines supports Turkish diplomacy. The first clear sign of government support came in 2003, one year after the AKP came to power, when liberalisation of the aviation sector strengthened Turkish Airlines' position nationally. The start-up of Anadolujet was one of the most striking examples, strengthening Turkish Airlines' position on the Istanbul–Ankara axis and opening up many destinations in Turkey's eastern provinces. This was fully in line with the wishes of the government.

Although the government's stake in Turkish Airlines had been decreased to 49 per cent following the partial privatisation of the airline, there is no doubt the government still has great influence on

Notwithstanding the crisis, Turkish Airlines continued to receive new aircraft, like this Airbus A321, in order to connect Turkey with Germany, one of its main markets. (Düsseldorf Airport)

Turkish Airlines introduced different logo jets to increase its visibility. (Jozef Mols)

This Boeing 737-800 was delivered in 2016. (Raymond Zammit)

In 2016, Turkish Airlines received its 300th aircraft: an Airbus A330-300. (Marianne Van Leuvenhaege)

When Turkish Airlines cooperated with Warner Bros Pictures to make *Batman v Superman: Dawn of Justice*, this Boeing 777 was painted accordingly. (John Taggart, Wikimedia Commons)

Chapter 11
Return to Profitability

After the several crises of 2015–16, Turkish Airlines took a series of steps towards a return to profitability, starting in early 2017. The new target was to reach a total of 69 million passengers. While Turkish Airlines had to cancel several international flights during the crisis, many of which were not reintroduced later, the airline could still enlarge its footprint thanks to a series of codeshare agreements. Furthermore, it was announced that Turkish Airlines would start flying to Aqaba in Jordan, Krasnodar in Russia (after the removal of Russian sanctions) and Freetown in Sierra Leone. Denpasar in Bali and Armenia were also planned.

On 1 May 2017, the *Middle East Economic Digest* (*MEED*) announced Turkish Airlines and Middle East Airlines (MEA) of Lebanon had signed a codeshare agreement. Turkish Airlines would place its code on MEA's twice-daily Istanbul–Beirut flights, and in return, MEA would place its code on Turkish Airlines' thrice-daily flights on the same route.[1] In October 2017, a codeshare agreement was signed between Turkish Airlines and Bahrain-based Gulf Air. Istanbul is a popular destination for Gulf nationals for both leisure and business activities. Prior to the agreement, both carriers offered a daily service between the two cities. Starting on 1 November 2017, the two flights would be operated under the new agreement. Earlier, in April 2017, Turkish Airlines had already signed a codeshare agreement with Copa Airlines, a subsidiary of Copa Holdings, SA. Both airlines were members of the Star Alliance. This way, Turkish Airlines could place its flight code on Copa flights between Panama City and Porto Alegre, Rio de Janeiro, Manaus, Belo Horizonte and São Paulo in Brazil, Santo Domingo and Punta Cana in the Dominican Republic, Guayaquil and Quito in Ecuador, San Salvador in El Salvador, Asunción in Paraguay and Lima in Peru. On the other hand, COPA placed its code on flights operated by Turkish Airlines between Panama and Istanbul. It was the intention that, once government approvals would be granted, Turkish Airlines would also place its code on COPA flights to Cancún, Mexico City and Guadalajara in Mexico, Managua in Nicaragua, San José in Costa Rica and Montevideo in Uruguay in order to expand the reach of these shared flights in the region.[2]

Turkish Airlines, given the financial discipline and dynamic demand management that had been applied since the beginning of 2017, could harvest the fruits of its efforts by the third quarter of the year. In Q3, the airline posted a record net profit for any Q3 in the airline's history, with a total amount of US$939m. The occupancy rate over the same period had reached 81.5 per cent, an increase of 17 per cent compared with the same period in the previous (crisis) year. Furthermore, Turkish Cargo contributed to the results. Its destinations had increased from 55 to 72 and cargo carried reached 294,000 tonnes, a 29 per cent increase compared with the previous year. Therefore, a further expansion of the cargo fleet was decided. The airline purchased three more Boeing 777 Freighters for delivery in September, October and December 2018.

On 11 November 2017, Turkish Airlines announced in a statement via the Public Disclosure Platform (KAP) of the Turkish government that it had established a real estate company with the name THY Airport Real Investment and Management Incorporation, with a capital of 50,000 Turkish Lira. This move can be considered in light of a possible opening of a new Istanbul airport.

In May 2018, it was announced Turkish Airlines had signed a codeshare agreement with Belavia Belarusian Airlines from Belarus, relating to flights between Istanbul and Minsk. In December 2018, a codeshare agreement was announced between Turkish and IndiGo from India. This was the first such agreement for IndiGo, which is the largest airline in India by market share. Moreover, IndiGo also signed a 'mutual cooperation' agreement with Turkish Airlines.[3]

Sponsorship deals also continued. On 14 September 2018, Turkish Airlines and Lega Basket Serie A, the top-tier professional basketball league in Italy, signed a sponsorship agreement, making the airline an official partner for the 2018–19 LBA Season.[4] Previously in 2018, the airline had been involved with the production of *Non-Transferable*, a romantic-comedy-travel movie by Brendan Bradley and Ashley Clements. The movie is about a young woman who books a surprise trip to Europe for her boyfriend just before he breaks up with her, and she searches the internet for a man who shares her ex's name to go with her. The producers worked with Turkish Airlines, the Turkish Ministry of Tourism and VIP Tourism Agency to fund the trip in exchange for featuring the airline, hotels and tourist attractions in the movie.[5]

In order to further expand its operations, Turkish Airlines once again had to modernise and enlarge its fleet. In July 2018, the airline took delivery of its first A321neo in 'Cabin Flex' configuration.[6] The aircraft is operated in a configuration of 20 seats in business class and 162 in economy class. Furthermore, the airline also placed orders for 25 Airbus A350XWBs and 30 Boeing 787-9 Dreamliners to be delivered between 2019 and 2023.[7]

By the end of 2018, it became clear that all the efforts by the Turkish Airlines management and staff had paid off. The crisis of 2015–16 could be forgotten. The airline reported that its net profit soared to US$745m. Revenues had increased by 58 per cent. The airline had served 75 million passengers, compared to 69 million in 2017.[8] The number of international passengers had increased by 9.6 per cent. Cargo/mail revenue went up by 25 per cent. At the same time, it was announced the airline set a target of 80 million passengers in 2019.

Turkish Airlines could only obtain such results by cashing in on a series of strengths. Turkey has one of the largest populations in Europe (80 million inhabitants), but its air travel market is relatively underpenetrated compared to other European countries. This offered significant growth potential for the aviation sector in a growing economy. Besides, the Istanbul hub of the airline attracts global transfer traffic. The airport is within narrow-body range of more than 40 per cent of global international traffic, and furthermore, the airline has a large global network. Obviously, if one compares Turkish Airlines with the big three Gulf carriers, Turkish Airlines only has a small footprint in Asia, but, on the other hand, has a stronger position in Europe. Of course, Turkish Airlines also offers high levels of connectivity. According to OAG on 31 December 2017, the airline has the highest connectivity by origin and destination pairs from Europe, the Middle East, Africa and the Far East to the rest of the world. From a management perspective, Turkish Airlines also has a very efficient cost structure in comparison to most full-service carriers.[9] The airline's relatively young fleet by comparison with those in its main regions of activity gives it an advantage in terms of fuel efficiency and customer appeal. As of October 2018, the average fleet age of Turkish Airlines was 7.7 years, compared with an average of 14 years for all European airlines, 10.9 years for Middle East airlines and 9.8 years for Asia Pacific airlines. Of course, Turkish Airlines also showed some weaknesses. Its Asia Pacific network is small versus the Gulf carriers with which it wants to compete. With strong ties with the Turkish government, the airline is vulnerable to political upheavals and conflicts. Furthermore, the currency crisis in Turkey, which was sparked by a diplomatic row between Turkey and the US, hit the Turkish Lira, demonstrating the vulnerability of Turkish Airlines to macro risks.[10]

The airline ordered three more Boeing 777F aircraft in order to cope with increased demand for cargo transportation. (Raymond Zammit)

Cargo/mail contributed in large part to the return to profitability in 2017–18. (Turkish Airlines)

Besides Boeings, Airbus cargo aircraft also contributed to the success of the cargo department. (Turkish Airlines)

With its modern and young fleet, Turkish Airlines could compete with other major carriers, including the Gulf carriers. (Turkish Airlines)

This leased Airbus A321-200 was painted in the 'The Year of Troy' special colours between 2018 and 2019. (Raymond Zammit)

Chapter 12
A New Era

Turkish Airlines managed to return to profitability in 2018. A year later, the airline would find a new opportunity to further approach its objectives. As the carrier was striving to further increase its connections, the opening of a new mega-airport on the European side of the Bosphorus was of utmost importance to the airline. Istanbul is a bridge between Europe on the one hand and Asia and Africa on the other. In the other direction, Istanbul offers access to Europe and the Americas for people living in Asia. Turkish Airlines used this strategic location to expand its international network.

Previously, Turkish Airlines flights left from the Atatürk Airport, one of the busiest airports in Europe. Since 2013, it has ranked among the five busiest airports in Europe by passenger traffic. As previously discussed, some of Turkish Airlines' aircraft were based at the Sabiha Gökçen Airport, which itself has a maximum terminal capacity of 25 million passengers. It was clear that Turkish Airlines' growth strategy was delayed because of constraints of the infrastructure. In 2017, the two Istanbul airports served more than 150 million passengers a year, while for comparison the three Paris-area airports only served around 100 million passengers.[1] Therefore, it was decided already in 2013 to construct a new airport, north of central Istanbul. A tender for construction and operation of the facility was held on 3 May 2013. The design team was led by London-based Grimshaw and Haptic and also included the Norway-based Nordic Office of Architecture.[2] The ground breaking ceremony took place on 7 June 2014. A first test landing took place on 20 June 2018. Testing of navigational and electronic systems with DHMI (Turkish government-owned aircraft used for calibration and testing) aircraft had begun on 14 May 2018.

The first stage of the project consists of the main terminal with an annual passenger capacity of 90 million people and an area of 15,500,000sq ft, making it the world's largest airport terminal under a single roof. There are two pairs of parallel runways connected to eight parallel taxiways to the west of the main terminal and the car park has a capacity of 12,000 vehicles. Additionally, the airport features three technical blocks for repairs, maintenance and fuelling, as well as an air traffic control tower in the shape of a tulip (the Turkish national flower). Furthermore, there are eight ramp control towers and hangars for cargo and general aviation aircraft. In a second stage, a third independent runway to the east of the main terminal will be added, as well as a fourth remote runway with an east–west heading and additional taxiways. In the third stage, a second passenger terminal with a capacity of 60 million annual passengers, as well as an additional runway and new support facilities should be built. A final fourth stage should see the construction of one more runway and the construction of several satellite terminals with a combined capacity of 50 million passengers. The target for completion is 2023, and by then, the airport should have six sets of runways and a total capacity of 150 million passengers. If fully expanded to a capacity of 200 million, the airport will exhibit four terminal buildings with interconnecting rail access.[3]

It is clear that the new Istanbul airport, the opening ceremony of which took place on 29 October 2018, offers great opportunities for Turkish Airlines in its quest for further expansion of the route network and the number of passengers carried. The first flight to take off from the new airport was Turkish Airlines flight TK2124 to the Turkish capital Ankara. Before the full transfer of the airport to its operators, all flights were exclusively operated by Turkish Airlines. The full transfer of all scheduled commercial passenger flights from Istanbul Atatürk Airport to the new airport took place on 6 April 2019. In preparation of that day, hundreds of aircraft made the short flight from south to north, while 14,000 ground vehicles were driven or transported across the city from the 'old' airport to the new Istanbul airport.

Obviously, such mega-projects have their own supporters and critics. The opening of Istanbul Airport, which will eventually be able to handle up to 200 million passengers a year, is not only a critical moment for the expansion of the airline, but it also symbolises President Erdogan's vision for his nation. According to some, Turkish Airlines had served as a soft power tool in his efforts to recast the country's place in the world.[4] The way in which Turkish Airlines received government support in the past, and also the opening of the new airport 'are examples of the way that political actors can support the aviation sector and turn it into a strategic tool'.[5] In his study, civil air transport specialist Julien Lebel states: 'A dynamic like this reflects the interest local governments have in the emergence of an aviation sector deemed vital to support their international ambitions. This is notably reflected by the significant financial and/or logistic support given to these airlines in the shape of state aid, tax relief, the inauguration of large airport infrastructures etc, which facilitates the emergence of major transit hubs. And so, more than just having a growth strategy, based on purely commercial parameters, these companies have extended their fleet and network in line with the interest of the political authorities which steer their development.'

The opening of the new airport was of great importance to Turkish Airlines, which was planning a further expansion of its fleet. On 26 June 2019, the first Boeing 787-9 Dreamliner from the airline's March 2018 order was delivered. At the same time, the airline was looking into receiving its orders for the Airbus A350-900 earlier than planned. Furthermore, it was announced the airline was also looking at the Airbus A220 and competing Embraer jets. Obviously, the grounding of the Boeing 737 MAX had created some problems, especially as, at the time of the grounding, Turkish Airlines had 11 737 MAX 8s and one 737 MAX 9 in its fleet. Additionally, delivery problems with the Airbus A321neo had arisen. And of course, politics played once again a role. President Erdogan had threatened to cancel orders for over 100 Boeing aircraft placed by Turkish Airlines due to his country's exclusion from the Lockheed Martin F-35 Lightning II programme.

Despite these problems, Turkish Airlines continued its policy of sponsoring large events in order to create maximum visibility. In February 2019, the airline had arranged to become a partial sponsor for League of Ireland First Division. In August of the same year, the airline reached agreement with Club Atlético River Plate, one of the biggest football clubs in Argentina.[6]

The opening of the new airport was a major step for Turkish Airlines but also demanded major logistic changes, resulting in sunk costs. Nevertheless, the airline could again publish some positive results for 2019. Its net profit reached US$788m, compared to US$753m the year before.

Inside the new Istanbul Airport. (Arne Müseler, Wikimedia Commons)

The duty-free shopping area at the new Istanbul Airport. (Matti Blume, Wikimedia Commons)

Landside of the new Istanbul Airport terminal. (Arne Müseler, Wikimedia Commons)

Turkish Airlines International CIP Lounge at the new airport. (Matti Blume, Wikimedia Commons)

Left: Inside the new terminal building. (Marianne Van Leuvenhaege)

Below: The control tower of the new Istanbul Airport. (Turkaviator on tr.wikimedia.org)

Istanbul Airport airside. (Marianne Van Leuvenhaege)

Istanbul Airport airside. (Marianne Van Leuvenhaege)

Turkish Airlines received its first Boeing 787-9 Dreamliner. (Adam Moreira, Wikimedia Commons)

Boeing 797 MAX aircraft parked at Istanbul Airport. (Turkish Airlines)

Chapter 13
More Challenges

If the opening of the new airport was a big challenge for Turkish Airlines, bigger challenges were looming. The beginning of 2019 seemed to be full of promises. Turkish Airlines enlarged its footprint, this time not by opening a new route, but by setting up a new subsidiary in Albania. In November 2011, the national flag carrier Albanian Airlines ceased to operate. Subsequently, the Albanian government had been searching for new investors to set up a successor. On 8 May 2017, Albanian Prime Minister Edi Rama announced the new airline would be set up with support from Turkish Airlines and President Erdogan. Air Albania was founded on 16 May 2018, by a consortium led by the Albanian and Turkish governments under a public-private partnership. Turkish Airlines, as founding partner, owns 49.12 per cent of the shares. The remaining 50.88 per cent is publicly traded, currently split between Albcontrol (a corporation owned by the Albanian government) and MDN Investment (a privately held company in Albania). The airline started its operations with an Airbus A319 and a Boeing 737-800, both on lease from Turkish Airlines. In its early days, destinations were limited to Turkey and Rome, Milan and Bologna in Italy.[1]

However, soon afterwards, the tides were turning. As for all airlines in the world, 2020 would become the toughest year in aviation history. Whereas in 2019, Turkish Airlines had transported over 74 million passengers, it had to celebrate its 87th anniversary on the ground. A new type of coronavirus pandemic spread all over the world and affected the whole aviation industry. Flights came to a standstill. On 2 April 2020, the airline suspended all international flights, and the majority of its domestic flights were also suspended.[2]

Turkish nationals, stranded abroad, were evacuated and brought back to their home country, although on some of these special flights, the cabin crew outnumbered the passengers.[3] Limited domestic flights were started up again on 4 June 2020, whereas a limited number of international flights took to the air starting on 10 June. As a direct result of the pandemic, Turkish Airlines only carried 28 million passengers in 2020, a decrease of 62 per cent compared to the previous year. This decrease was the most noticeable on international flights, with a 67.8 per cent decrease, while the number of transfer passengers went down by 70.3 per cent. Domestic passenger numbers went down by 50.5 per cent.[4]

After the grounding of its fleet because of the COVID-19 pandemic, Turkish Airlines broke new ground globally by including 50 of its passenger aircraft in the 25 aircraft cargo fleet. Turkish Cargo registered the biggest breakthrough during the pandemic and many of the wide-body passenger aircraft in the fleet were used for cargo transport to meet growing demand. The airline carried 50,000 tonnes of medications and medical supplies in 2020, but increased demand for air cargo services as a result of increases in e-commerce also played a role. As a result, the airline could boost its market share in cargo transport and carry one out of every 20 shipments worldwide in 2020.[5] During 2020, cargo unit revenues therefore rose by 66 per cent, resulting in revenues of US$2.7bn.[6] Thanks to the contribution of the cargo unit, Turkish Airlines posted a loss of only US$836m for 2020.[7]

At the end of 2020, the new Istanbul Airport made history by serving the most passengers in Europe, leaving London Heathrow and Frankfurt behind. The primary driver of this success was Turkish Airlines, which continued to serve more destinations than its competitors.[8]

Turkish Airlines' subsidiary Air Albania was also hit by the pandemic. The airline carried out 73 evacuation flights in 2020, transporting some 10,500 Albanian citizens from major European cities to their home country, and some 6,000 foreign citizens were flown from Albania to their country of residence. In July 2020, the airline could resume limited flights between Tirana and Istanbul, Rome, Milan, Bologna, Pisa, Verona and Bergamo.[9]

Responding to increased demand for cargo transportation, Turkish Airlines decided to establish an independent cargo airline. Whereas Turkish Cargo was previously a sub-brand of Turkish Airlines, the department would now become a fully independent company, owned by Turkish Airlines.[10] This should allow the airline to speed up decision making. At the same time, it was planned that the new airline would become the fifth largest cargo airline by the end of 2023. Thanks to its independent status, the new airline would also be able to join its own international freight alliances.[11]

The COVID-19 pandemic was a major challenge for Turkish Airlines, but it was not the only one. The worldwide grounding of the Boeing 737 MAX also caused headaches. At the time of the grounding, the airline had received a total of 12 aircraft of this type in its fleet. These were part of an order for a total of 75 aircraft. Turkish Airlines indeed saw the aircraft as vital to its long-term narrow-body requirements. In December 2020, the airline reached a settlement with Boeing over compensation for the grounding and the financial losses incurred. Of course, the airline was eager to put the aircraft back in service, but it had to wait till it was cleared by the Turkish Directorate General of Civil Aviation. This happened by the end of 2020 – followed by European Union Aviation Safety Agency (EASA) clearing in November 2020 – and it was expected the airline would resume Boeing 737 MAX flights by April 2021. In the meantime, however, Turkish Airlines revised its outstanding order and agreed with Boeing to reduce the order by ten aircraft. In addition, a further 40 Boeing 737 MAX firm orders would be turned into options. Delivery of the remaining 13 aircraft would be rescheduled because of 'operational reasons' related to the COVID-19 pandemic.[12] In the meantime, one 737 MAX (TC-LCA) returned to service on 15 April 2021. A second one (TC-LCE) would soon follow.[13]

By the end of 2020, Turkish Airlines also started operating its newly delivered initial pair of Airbus A350-900s on domestic routes.[14] Meanwhile, it was announced that the airline had reached a deal with Airbus to restructure its order backlog. It is uncertain how many more A350s Turkish Airlines will take delivery of in the next months, given the impact of COVID-19 on global travel. In a stock market announcement on 23 October, the airline had indicated that 'undelivered orders had been rescheduled in line with the airline's operational and financial capabilities'. Aside from the A350s, Turkish Airlines also had 71 A321-200neos due from Airbus.[15]

Very recently, Turkish Airlines' results for the first half of 2021 became available. Between January and July 2021, the airline had carried 20.1 million passengers and the load factor had decreased by 16.2 per cent to 64.4 per cent. However, cargo/mail carried during the January–July 2021 period had increased by 26 per cent compared to the first half of 2019.[16] Comparing the six-month period of 2021 with the first half of 2019, revenues were down 33.2 per cent to US$4bn.[17] By the end of the first half of 2021, the airline had a fleet of 373 aircraft.

Notwithstanding all problems, the airline remains positive about the future. In an interview with *anna.aero*, Ilker Ayci, chairman of the board and executive committee of Turkish Airlines, gave his comments on the last five years of operations.[18] He said: 'After a five-year period of tremendous growth, we met a global pandemic crisis. The first priority at the present time is crisis management. Secondly, we should also be ready to plan for the post-pandemic period. I'm doing both with my team.' Impressively, Turkish Airlines had maintained a load factor of more than 60 per cent during the pandemic. 'Exemplary hygiene standards and safe travel measures give confidence to passengers, and they have responded very positively. We have the fourth largest network in the world and serve more countries (127) than any other airline,' he added.

To further underline his optimism, Turkish Airlines revealed it would add new flights to Cebu City in the Philippines 'based on market conditions'.[19] Furthermore, according to the CTC – Corporate

Travel Community, the airline stated it plans to commence scheduled services to A Coruña, Abha, Aswan, Juba, Nantes, Palermo, Port Sudan and Sialkot 'based on aircraft availability and market conditions'. Earlier, the airline had already recommenced flights to Urumieh, Vancouver, New York, Newark, Turkistan as well as Fergana and Urgench in Uzbekistan.[20]

With such optimistic words, and, given the excellent performance Turkish Airlines showed in previous years, indeed since the deregulation of air traffic in Turkey, one can only hope the airline will manage to reach its targets. Turkish Airlines can be congratulated on its past achievements and it is hoped it will continue to prosper in the near future.

Turkish Airlines set up Air Albania, together with the Albanian government, and leased this Airbus A319 to the new airline. (Albinfo, Wikimedia Commons)

This Boeing 737-800 was also leased from Turkish Airlines to Air Albania. (Therealkuba11, Wikimedia Commons)

During the COVID-19 pandemic, Turkish Cargo transported a great amount of medical supplies. (Turkish Cargo)

Turkish Cargo became an independent company, owned by Turkish Airlines. (Turkish Cargo)

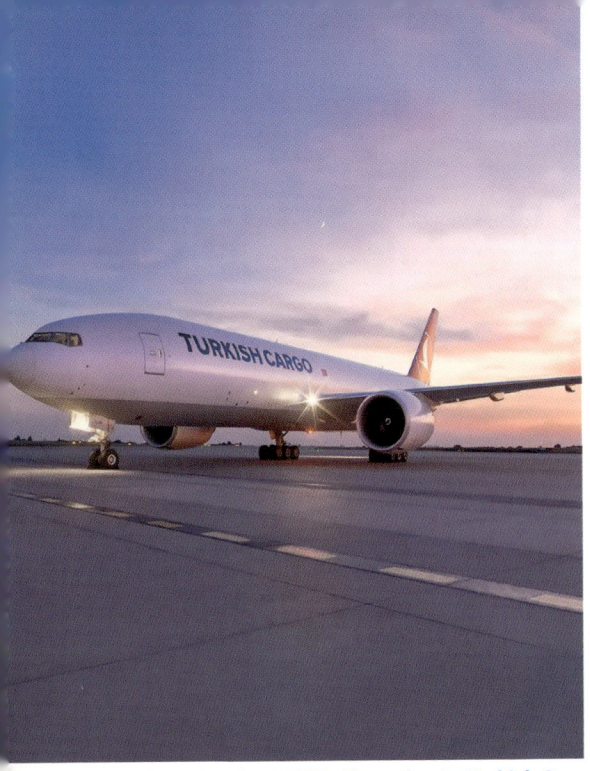

Above left: During the COVID-19 pandemic, Turkish Cargo contributed greatly to the fiscal results of Turkish Airlines. (Turkish Airlines)

Above right: Turkish Airlines' maintenance department. (Turkish Airlines)

Below: A new Airbus A350 at the new Istanbul Airport. (Ogulcan Bingöl)

Appendix 1
Incidents and Accidents

(Based upon information from the Accident Safety Network)

On 17 February 1959, a Vickers Viscount Type 793 (TC-SEV) operating a charter flight and carrying the Turkish Prime Minister Adnan Menderes and a governmental delegation to London crashed in dense fog on approach to London Gatwick. Nine of the 16 passengers and five of the eight crew members lost their lives. The prime minister, who was sitting in the back of the aircraft, survived.

On 23 September 1961, a Fokker F27-100 (TC-TAY) operating flight 835 crashed at Karanlık Tepe in the province of Ankara on approach to Esenboğa Airport. All four crew members and 24 of the 25 passengers were killed.

On 8 March 1962, a Fairchild F-27 (TC-KOP) crashed into the Taurus Mountains on approach to Adana Şakirpaşa Airport. All three crew members and all eight passengers on board died.

On 3 February 1964, a Douglas C-47 (TC-ETI) on a domestic cargo flight flew into terrain while approaching Esenboğa Airport in Ankara. All three crew members on board were killed.

On 2 February 1969, a Vickers Viscount Type 794 (TC-SET) crashed on approach to Esenboğa Airport. There were no casualties.

On 26 January 1974, a Fokker F28-1000 (TC-JAO) performing flight 301 crashed shortly after taking off from Izmir Cumaovası Airport due to over-rotation and icing on the wings. The aircraft disintegrated and caught fire. Four of the five crew members and 62 of the 68 passengers were killed.

On 3 March 1974, a McDonnell Douglas DC-10 (TC-JAV) operating flight 981 crashed into Ermenonville Forest in Fontaine-Chaalis (Oise, France) due to explosive decompression. All 335 passengers and 11 crew were killed. Most of the passengers had been rebooked on this flight because of a strike at British Airways. The main cause of the accident was a design fault on the cargo doors of the aircraft, which led to incomplete engagement of the door-locking mechanism on the aircraft and consequently the opening of one of the doors in flight.

On 30 January 1975, a Fokker F-28-1000 (TC-JAP) operating flight 345 crashed into the Sea of Marmara during final night instrument approach to Istanbul Yeşilköy Airport. On a first landing attempt, an electrical power failure at the airport at that very moment forced the crew to initiate a missed approach. A few seconds later, the emergency generator restored the runway lights. The pilot elected to remain VFR (Visual Flight Rules) under an altitude of 790ft. The crew asked for permission to land while positioning for another approach. However, because another aircraft (a Pan American Boeing 707) was about to take off, air traffic control ordered the Turkish crew to fly an extended downwind leg. When air traffic control tried to establish communication with the Fokker aircraft, there was no answer. All four crew members and all 38 passengers perished.

On 19 September 1976, a Boeing 727-200 (TC-JBH) operating flight 452 from Istanbul to Antalya Airport struck high ground at Karatepe during an attempted landing in Isparta instead of Antalya Airport because of pilot error. It is possible the pilot mistook the lights of a highway north of Isparta for the Antalya boulevard near to the Antalya airport. All eight crew members and 146 people on board were killed.

On 23 December 1979, a Fokker F28-1000 (TC-JAT) on a flight from Samsun to Esenboğa Airport struck a hill in Kuyumcuköy village in Çubuk (Ankara), 20 miles northeast of its destination airport, due to severe turbulence. The crew had deviated from the localiser course while on ILS (Instrument Landing System). Three of the four crew members and 38 of the 48 passengers on board were killed.

On 16 January 1983, a Boeing 727-200 (TC-JBR) operating flight 158 landed about 160ft short of the runway at Esenboğa Airport in driving snow, subsequently breaking up and catching fire. All seven crew members survived, whereas 47 of the 60 passengers died.

On 29 December 1994, a Boeing 737-400 (TC-JES) operating flight 278 crashed during its final approach to Van Ferit Melen Airport in driving snow. Five of the seven crew members and 52 of the 69 passengers died.

On 7 April 1999, a Boeing 737-400 (TC-JEP) on a repositioning flight crashed near Ceyhan (Adana) shortly after take-off from Adana Airport. The aircraft was on its way to Adana to pick up Turkish pilgrims on their way to Mecca. The weather was poor when the aircraft crashed nine minutes after take-off. The wreckage was found to have been scattered over a 500sq ft area. All six crew members perished. Analysis of data shows that severe weather conditions may have contributed to the crash. The pitot static anti-ice system was probably not activated during preparation for flight because of missed checklist items. The crew had failed to recognise the cause of an erratic airspeed indication. The presence of cabin crew in the cockpit probably distracted the attention of the cockpit crew.

On 8 January 2003, an Avro RJ-100 (TC-THG) operating flight 634 crashed on approach to Diyarbakır Airport in heavy fog. The aircraft impacted the ground and broke up short of the runway. All five crew members and 70 of the 80 passengers on board died.

On 3 October 2006, Turkish Airlines flight 1476 en route from Tirana (Albania) to Istanbul was hijacked in Greek airspace by an unarmed Turkish citizen, Hakan Ekinci. He threatened to blow up the aircraft if the pilot would not fly to Italy. The hijacker surrendered after a forced landing in Brindisi (Italy).

On 25 February 2009, a Boeing 737-800 (TC-JGE) on flight 1951 crashed during approach on autopilot to Amsterdam Schiphol Airport. A faulty altimeter caused the aircraft to throttle the engines back to idle and the crew subsequently failed to react quickly enough, which resulted in an unrecoverable stall and crash. The same aircraft had experienced problems with the altimeter twice before. Of the 135 people on board, nine people including three pilots were killed. Eighty-six passengers were transported to local hospitals, some of them in critical condition. Boeing was instructed to warn its clients about possible problems with altimeters in this type of aircraft.

On 3 March 2015, an Airbus A330-300 (TC-JOC) operating flight 726 departed the runway upon landing at Tribhuvan International Airport in Kathmandu, Nepal. The aircraft had aborted the first approach to Runway 02 and had gone around from about minimum descent altitude due to fog. On the second landing attempt, the aircraft was severely damaged when its nose gear collapsed, causing damage to the fuselage and both wings. One of the wheels touched down off the runway, the tyre burst and the aircraft subsequently veered left. All 227 passengers and 11 crew members escaped without major injuries. Four passengers received minor injuries during the evacuation.

On 25 April 2015, an Airbus A320-200 (TC-JPE) operating flight 1878 was severely damaged in a landing accident at Istanbul Atatürk Airport. After a first landing attempt (which resulted in the wing touching the runway and the collapse of the right main gear) and a go-around, the aircraft landed but rolled right just before touchdown, causing the right engine and wing to contact the runway. All on board were successfully evacuated without any injuries.

On 16 January 2017, Turkish Airlines 6491, a Boeing 747-412F (TC-MCL) operated by MyCargo (formerly known as ACT Airlines) on a flight from Hong Kong to Bishkek (Kyrgyzstan) on behalf of Turkish Airlines, crashed into a residential area upon landing in Manas International Airport in Bishkek, killing all four crew members and 35 people on the ground. Eight people on the ground were taken to hospital. At the time of landing, adverse weather conditions were reported. Turkish Airlines released a statement that neither the aircraft nor the crew were theirs, calling it an ACT-accident. However, as the flight was operated under a Turkish Airlines flight number, it was a Turkish Airlines flight under IATA rules. Later analysis of the black boxes revealed that missing control of the crew over the aircraft position in relation to the glideslope during automatic approach, conducted at night in bad weather conditions, was the main cause of the accident. The measures to perform a go-around were not taken in due time, resulting in an impact with terrain beyond the end of the active runway.

On 21 November 2019, a Boeing 737-800 operating flight 467 suffered a nose gear collapse while attempting for the second time to land in heavy crosswinds at Odessa International Airport in Ukraine. According to the *Daily Mirror*, panic erupted. The aircraft skidded off the runway and stopped in a field. All passengers and crew were deplaned using emergency slides. There were no injuries.

An Airbus A320 prior to delivery. (Turkish Airlines)

Appendix 2
Turkish Airlines' Fleet Details

(Based upon information from the airline and from Planespotters.net)

Historic fleet

Aircraft Type	Total Number Used	First Introduction	Last Removed from Fleet
Douglas DC-9-10	1	1967	1973
Douglas DC-9-30	10	1968	1995
Douglas DC-10-10	3	1972	1989
Airbus A 310-200	11	1985	2008
Airbus A310-300F	4	1988	2015
Airbus A310-300	4	1989	2015
Boeing 737-400	32	1991	2013
Boeing 737-500	2	1992	2004
Airbus A 340-300	9	1993	2020
British Aerospace Avro RJ 100	10	1993	2007
Douglas DC-10-30	1	1993	1993
Airbus A319-200	35	1996	2020
British Aerospace Avro RJ 70	4	1996	2005
Boeing 737-800	50	1998	2021
Douglas MD-90	2	1998	1998
Airbus A321-100	2	2004	2007
Airbus A300B4	2	2005	2006
Airbus A321-200	7	2005	2020
Douglas MD-83	3	2005	2006
Airbus A319-100	7	2006	2019
Airbus A330-200	10	2009	2020
Boeing 737-400	4	2009	2019
Boeing 777-300ER	6	2009	2011
Airbus A330-300	3	2010	2020
Airbus A330-200F	1	2013	2013

Current fleet

Aircraft Type	In Service	Parked	Total	On Order
Airbus A319	6		6	
Airbus A320	11		11	
Airbus A321	81	16	97	
Airbus A330	50	12	62	
Airbus A350XWB	5		5	
Boeing 737	67	5	72	8
Boeing 777	36	5	41	
Boeing 787	15		15	2

A Boeing 777-300ER. (John Taggart on Wikimedia Commons)

Appendix 3

Notes and References

Chapter 1
1. For more information about the start-up of the Turkish Air Force, read 'The Establishment Years', Republic of Turkey, Ministry of National Defence, Turkish Air Force
2. 'Vecihi Hürkuş', en.wikipedia.org
3. 'Vecihi Hürkuş', military.wikia.org
4. 'Turkish Airlines', en.wikipedia.org
5. 'Turkish Airlines is 88 Years Old', *Railly News,* Ankara (21 May 2021)

Chapter 2
1. 'Turkish Airlines', Investor Relations Turkish Airlines, https://investor.turkishairlines.com
2. 'Turkish Airlines', en.wikipedia.org
3. 'Turkish Airlines', Investor Relations Turkish Airlines
4. Turkish Airlines, 'Our Story', turkishairlines.com

Chapter 3
1. 'Cyprus', en.wikipedia.org
2. 'Turkish Invasion of Cyprus', en.wikipedia.org
3. 'Bloody Christmas 1963', en.wikipedia.org
4. '1974 Turkish Invasion of Cyprus', en.wikipedia.org
5. 'Cyprus Turkish Airlines', Allairlineinfos.blogspot.com
6. 'Cyprus Turkish Airlines', en.wikipedia.org

Chapter 4
1. '1980 Turkish Coup d'État', en.wikipedia.org
2. Okuyucu, Ayşe, 'Tourism Development in Turkey: Development Process, Challenges and Patterns', *International Journal of Social Science*, Volume 6, Issue 7, pp. 815–827 (July 2013)
3. Tamir, Cetin, 'Estimating the Economic Effects of Deregulation: Evidence from the Turkish Airline Industry', Yıldız Technical University and Uludağ University, researchgate.net (2010)
4. Gerede Ender, Dr, 'The Evolution of Turkish Airline Industry: Significant Developments and the Impact of 1983 Liberalization', Anadolu University, Eskişehir, researchgate.net (2010)
5. Tamir, Cetin, 'Estimating the Economic Effects of Deregulation: Evidence from the Turkish Airline Industry', Yıldız Technical University and Uludağ University, researchgate.net (2010)
6. Gerede Ender, Dr, 'The Evolution of Turkish Airline Industry: Significant Developments and the Impact of 1983 Liberalization', Anadolu University, Eskişehir, researchgate.net (2010)
7. 'Torosair', de.wikipedia.org

Chapter 5

1. European Commission 'Turkey – Membership Status', ec.europe.eu (January 2021) Gerede Ender, Dr, 'The Evolution of Turkish Airline Industry: Significant Developments and the Impact of 1983 Liberalization', Anadolu University, Eskişehir (2010)
2. 'Turkish Airlines', en.wikipedia.org
3. Gerede Ender, Dr, 'The Evolution of Turkish Airline Industry: Significant Developments and the Impact of 1983 Liberalization', Anadolu University, Eskişehir (2010)
4. 'Turkish Airlines Inc', encyclopedia.com
5. 'Turkish Airlines Inc Company Profile', www.referenceforbusiness.com

Chapter 6

1. Gerede Ender, Dr, 'The Evolution of Turkish Airline Industry: Significant Developments and the Impact of 1983 Liberalization', Anadolu University, Eskişehir (2010)
2. 'Turkish Airlines', en.wikipedia.org
3. Sengur, Ferhan Kuyucak, 'Public-Private Partnership in Airports – The Turkish Experience', Eskişehir Technical University, researchgate.net (2010)
4. 'Turkish Airlines Inc Company Profile', www.referenceforbusiness.com

Chapter 7

1. Gerede Ender and Orhan Gamze, 'A study of the Strategic Responses of the Turkish Airline Companies to the Deregulation in Turkey', *Journal of Marketing Research*, Vol 4, Anadolu University, Eskişehir, Turkey (2013)
2. Ibid
3. Peksatici, Ozge, 'Competitive Strategies of Airline Companies Operating in the Turkish Domestic Aviation Market'. Institute Of Social Sciences, Bahçeşehir University, Turkey (2010)
4. Gerede Ender, Dr, 'The Evolution of Turkish Airline Industry: Significant Developments and the Impact of 1983 Liberalization', Anadolu University, Eskişehir (2010)

Chapter 8

1. Gerede Ender and Orhan Gamze, 'A study of the Strategic Responses of the Turkish Airline Companies to the Deregulation in Turkey', *Journal of Marketing Research*, Vol 4, Anadolu University, Eskişehir, Turkey (2013)
2. Ozcelik, Eren, 'Turkish Airlines vs Pegasus Airlines', Istanbul Technical University (2018)
3. Pegasus Airlines, 'About Us', flypgs.com
4. 'Turkish Airlines Flight 1951', en.wikipedia.org
5. 'Turkish Airlines Flight 1951 Crash', Timenote.info (February 2009)
6. 'Turkish Airlines Flight 1951', en.wikipedia.org
7. Hamby, Chris, 'A Decade Later, Dutch Officials Publish a Study Critical of Boeing', *The New York Times* (21 January 2020)
8. Hamby, Chris, 'Boeing Refuses to Cooperate with New Inquiry into Deadly Crash', *The New York Times* (10 February 2020)
9. 'Boeing Boss Refuses to Discuss Turkish Airlines Crash with Dutch Authorities', *NL Times* (30 January 2020)
10. 'US Pressured Dutch Safety Board to Downplay Tech Faults in 2009 Turkish Airlines Crash', *NL Times* (21 January 2020)

11. 'Turkish Airlines Flight 1951', en.wikipedia.org
12. Boncuck, May, 'Boeing Cover Up: Turkish Airlines Flight 1951', Moviboncukblogspot.com (21 January 2020)

Chapter 9

1. 'Turkish Airlines Becomes Number 1 in the World to the Most Countries Worldwide', *Businesswire* and *Flyertalk* (14 November 2012)
2. 'Marseille Lands Turkish Airlines Partnership', *Goal* (3 September 2013)
3. 'Turkish Airlines Launches Partnership with German Soccer Club Borussia Dortmund', *IndiaTelevision* (26 April 2013)
4. 'Turkish Airlines Places its Biggest Order Ever with Airbus', www.aviation24.be (15 March 2013)
5. 'Turkish Airlines Joins UEFA Euro 2016 as Airline Partner', *Financial Express India* (18 December 2015)
6. 'Best Connected Airline Hubs by Region Revealed', *anna.aero* (29 July 2015)

Chapter 10

1. 'Europe's Leading Airline to Introduce Batman's Gotham City and Superman's Metropolis as Newest U.S. Destinations via Sponsorship', Turkish Airlines Media Relations (March 2016)
2. Lebel, Julien, 'Turkish Airlines: An International Strategic Instrument of Turkey', *Etudes de l'Ifri* (April 2020)
3. Ibid
4. Ibid
5. 'Turkey's coup attempt: What you need to know', *BBC News* (17 July 2016)
6. US Embassy in Ankara (16 July 2016)
7. 'Turkish Airlines posts loss of $644m, revises target', Hurriyetdailynews (22 August 2016)
8. 'Massiver Gewinn-Einbruch bei Turkish Airlines', *Frankfurter Rundschau* (20 August 2016)
9. 'Russia-Turkey Relations', en.wikipedia.org
10. Lebel, Julien, 'Turkish Airlines: An International Strategic Instrument of Turkey', *Etudes de l'Ifri* (April 2020)
11. Turkish Airlines press release (25 July 2016)
12. 'Turkish Airlines Names Jets After Coup Plot Resistance Sites', *Hürriyetdailynews* (16 August 2016)
13. Lebel, Julien, 'Turkish Airlines: An International Strategic Instrument of Turkey', *Etudes de l'Ifri* (April 2020)

Chapter 11

1. 'Lebanon's Middle East Airlines and Istanbul-based Turkish Airlines will codeshare beginning May 15', *Middle East Economic Digest* (1 May 2017)
2. 'Copa Airlines and Turkish Airlines start codeshare flights between Europe and Latin America', Copa Air press release (28 April 2017)
3. 'IndiGo signs codeshare agreement with Turkish Airlines', *Moneycontrol* (22 December 2018)
4. 'Turkish Airlines', en.wikipedia.org
5. Linnell, Christine, 'Non-Transferable', *What's Trending* (23 February 2017)
6. 'Airbus Delivers the first A321neo in Cabin Flex configuration to Turkish Airlines', Airbus press release (13 July 2018)
7. 'Turkish Airlines selects A350 XWB, lifting its fleet to new heights', Airbus Press Release (9 March 2018)

8. 'Turkish Airlines' profits surge to 4 billion Turkish Lira in 2018', *Hürriyetdailynews* (5 March 2019)
9. 'Turkish Airlines SWOT: more growth for the Istanbul superconnector', CAPA Centre for Aviation, (12 October 2018)
10. Ibid

Chapter 12
1. 'Istanbul Airport', en.wikipedia.org
2. Ibid
3. Ibid
4. Pitel, Laura, 'Turkish Airlines flying the flag for Erdogan', *Financial Times* (7 November 2018)
5. Lebel, Julien, 'Developing a common civil aviation strategy: vital to guarantee Europe's interests in the international arena', *Foundation Robert Schuman*, European Issues, No 482 (4 September 2018)
6. Anadolu Press Agency (3 August 2019)
7. 'Consolidated Financial Statements as at and for the Year Ended 31 December 2019', Turkish Airlines Investor Relations (5 March 2020)

Chapter 13
1. 'Air Albania', en.wikipedia.org
2. Hofmann, Kurt, 'Turkish Airlines suspends all international flights', *Routesonline* (2 April 2020)
3. 'Turkish Airlines Annual Report 2020', Turkish Airlines Investor Relations (January 2021)
4. Ibid
5. Ibid
6. Ibid
7. Dunn, Graham, 'Turkish Airlines posts $836m net loss for 2020 despite freight boost', *Flight Global* (2 March 2021)
8. 'Turkish Airlines Annual Report 2020', Turkish Airlines Investor Relations (January 2021)
9. Ibid
10. 'Turkish Airlines Establishes Cargo Company', Istanbul Gelisim University (1 June 2020)
11. Versleijen, John, 'Turkish Airlines Verzelfstandigt Vrachtdivisie', *Luchtvaartnieuws NL* (1 December 2020)
12. 'Turkish Airlines verkleint oder voor Boeing 737 MAX', *Luchtvaartnieuws NL* (17 April 2021)
13. 'THY'nin "B737 MAX" uçaklan 2 yildan sonra gökyüzüne yeniden dönüyor', *AA Sirket Haberleri* (9 April 2021)
14. Keminski-Morrow, David, 'Turkish A350s quietly begin operations as crisis saps profits', *Flight Global* (November 2020)
15. 'Turkish Airlines has reached an agreement with Airbus', *Tourism International* (28 October 2020)
16. 'Traffic Results for the period of January – July 2021', Turkish Airlines Investor Relations (10 August 2021)
17. 'Turkish Airlines Stems Losses, Builds Up Cargo Business', *Aviation Week Network* (11 August 2021)
18. 'FTE-APEX Virtual Expo 2021 – Turkish Airlines' 'new istanbul hub allowing us to invite more airlines to fly to Istanbul', *anna.aero* (26 May 2021)
19. 'Traffic Results for the period of January–July 2021', Turkish Airlines Investor Relations (10 August 2021)
20. 'Turkish Airlines planning 17 new international destinations after adding six in 1H2021', *Corporate Travel Community* (12 August 2021)